Cambridge Elements ≡

Elements in Ethics
edited by
Ben Eggleston
University of Kansas
Dale E. Miller
Old Dominion University, Virginia

AQUINAS'S ETHICS

Thomas M. Osborne Jr.
University of St Thomas, Houston

T0364230

CAMBRIDGE
UNIVERSITY PRESS

CAMBRIDGE
UNIVERSITY PRESS

University Printing House, Cambridge CB2 8BS, United Kingdom

One Liberty Plaza, 20th Floor, New York, NY 10006, USA

477 Williamstown Road, Port Melbourne, VIC 3207, Australia

314–321, 3rd Floor, Plot 3, Splendor Forum, Jasola District Centre,
New Delhi – 110025, India

79 Anson Road, #06–04/06, Singapore 079906

Cambridge University Press is part of the University of Cambridge.

It furthers the University's mission by disseminating knowledge in the pursuit of
education, learning, and research at the highest international levels of excellence.

www.cambridge.org
Information on this title: www.cambridge.org/9781108706551
DOI: 10.1017/9781108581325

First published 2020

A catalogue record for this publication is available from the British Library.

ISBN 978-1-108-70655-1 Paperback
ISSN 2516-4031 (online)
ISSN 2516-4023 (print)

Aquinas's Ethics

Elements in Ethics

DOI: 10.1017/9781108581325
First published online: April 2020

Thomas M. Osborne Jr.
University of St. Thomas, Houston

Author for correspondence: Thomas M. Osborne Jr, osborntm@stthom.edu

Abstract: This Element provides an account of Thomas Aquinas's moral philosophy that emphasizes the intrinsic connection between happiness and the human good, human virtue, and the precepts of practical reason. Human beings by nature have an end to which they are directed and concerning which they do not deliberate – namely, happiness. Humans achieve this end by performing good human acts, which are produced by the intellect and the will and perfected by the relevant virtues. These virtuous acts require that the agent grasps the relevant moral principles and uses them in particular cases.

Keywords: Aquinas, Happiness, Virtue, Natural Law, Practical Reasoning

ISBNs: 9781108706551 (PB), 9781108581325 (OC)
ISSNs: 2516-4031 (online), 2516-4023 (print)

Contents

1 Introduction

Thomas Aquinas's ethical theory is difficult to classify according to the standard contemporary philosophical criteria. Even though his work partially inspired the late twentieth-century revival of virtue ethics as an alternative to Kantian deontology and utilitarianism or consequentialism, his philosophy shares or prefigures features of these two systems (MacIntyre 1992). For instance, along with philosophers who are influenced by Kant, Aquinas emphasizes that moral rules are necessary for our moral reasoning and that humans are free to follow or depart from such rules. On the other hand, Aquinas resembles the consequentialists and utilitarians in his emphasis on the end in his account of moral goodness. Rules should be followed not for their own sake but because they indicate how the good is attained. I will show that Aquinas brings together three elements of moral theories that are often kept apart by modern and contemporary philosophers – namely, 1) the intrinsic connection between happiness and the human good, 2) the central role of human virtue in achieving this good, and 3) the importance of moral rules, including certain rules that apply to every act or in every relevant situation.

There are special difficulties that must be overcome when discussing Aquinas's moral philosophy, and perhaps to some extent the moral philosophy of any medieval theologian. This Introduction addresses perhaps the three greatest difficulties, which are his indebtedness to previous authors, his theological context, and his understanding of moral philosophy as a distinct science of human action. Aquinas does not pretend to develop an original ethical system. Like much of his philosophy in general, Aquinas's ethics is rooted in a variety of earlier philosophical traditions and is worked out primarily in the context of his theology, which is part of the wider scholastic attempt to develop a theological science that qualifies as an Aristotelian science. Although many modern and contemporary philosophers write works that purport to be comprehensible apart from a historical or religious tradition, or even a social context, Aquinas and other medieval theologians do not pretend to write such completely original secular philosophy. Aquinas cannot be understood in isolation from previous Christian writers and the ancient philosophy that is found in their works. However, Aquinas also knows Latin pagan writers such as Cicero and Seneca, and the then growing body of work that was translated into Latin from Greek and Arabic. In such an intellectual context, ethics is a distinct branch of moral science about human action. Aquinas does not develop his own completely original science but uses previous writers to provide what he thinks is an adequate account of such a topic.

Aquinas's understanding of the scientific nature of moral philosophy and theology also needs explanation. Aquinas's academic work was carried out largely in universities that taught all branches of the sciences that were then known or thought to be known, including the science of theology, as well as in religious houses of study that taught many of the same subjects. Contemporary readers might be confused by his use of the Latin word *scientia* to describe theology and moral philosophy. We are using the common but potentially misleading translation of this word as "science." According to Aristotle and his followers, a science is generally speaking a habit of knowing conclusions that are demonstrated from better-known explanatory principles. Theology is a science in this sense. The principles of theology are the articles of faith, which are in the Bible and passed down through the Christian tradition. These are known only through revelation. But in order to defend and more fully understand revelation, Aquinas uses the philosophical sciences, which are based on principles that are known to human reason apart from revelation. Moral philosophy is one of many philosophical sciences.

In the thirteenth century, the philosophical sciences were taught in a separate and preparatory arts faculty at the University of Paris or in other institutional settings. Only some students continued to study theology under such teachers as Aquinas, who generally were the best philosophers of the period, even though they were primarily theologians. Their theology presupposes philosophy. Additionally, it rests on and develops philosophical principles and arguments. Even though the theologians were skilled philosophers, it should be kept in mind that by interest and occupation their acquisition of philosophical science was subordinated to theology.

The historical background to Aquinas sheds light on how and why he integrates material from a wide variety of philosophical sources. His era is distinctive not only for its religious context but also for the way in which it was influenced by a variety of intellectual currents (Torrell 2005, 63–85). Aquinas, alongside many of his contemporaries, drew on pagan, Christian, Islamic, and Jewish thinkers. His generation was the first in the Latin West to have access to virtually all of Aristotle's complete works in Latin translation. Theologians who worked in Latin had to integrate this new knowledge into an already well-developed theological tradition. Previous generations had relied on a Christian intellectual tradition that was rooted in the writings of earlier Christians such as Ambrose of Milan and Augustine of Hippo. These early Latin Christian writers were influenced philosophically primarily by Neoplatonic and Stoic philosophers rather than by Aristotelianism. Augustine was not only the most important theologian for Latin Christianity but a philosopher of the highest order. However, he had only a scanty knowledge of Aristotle's works.

A more logically rigorous theological approach developed in the late twelfth and early thirteenth centuries. Before the early thirteenth century, Western theologians had little direct access to Aristotle's works, pagan commentaries on it, and the later Arabic Aristotelian tradition. They knew the pagan philosophy that could be found in the Church Fathers, some more philosophical Roman writers such as Cicero and Seneca, and a few Latin translations by figures such as Boethius. In particular, Cicero's work was a central part of the education of Aquinas and his predecessors, and the moral philosophy of Cicero's more or less Stoic *De Officiis* was absorbed by many Christian authors. Consequently, Christian theologians learned and developed a moral philosophy that, under the influence of Stoicism, emphasized right reason, living in accordance with nature, and the four cardinal virtues of prudence, justice, courage, and temperance.

Aquinas's teacher Albert the Great was among the first to take into account the newly translated works of Aristotle and, in particular, his *Nicomachean Ethics*, which previously had been available only in the first three books. One of Aquinas's earliest professional tasks was to put in order Albert's remarks on the *Nicomachean Ethics*, and in his last years he wrote his own detailed commentary on it, which has become one of the most successful attempts to explain Aristotle's moral philosophy. There are differences between Aquinas's reading of Aristotle and that of many contemporary scholars. Aquinas inherited a living tradition of commentary on, and reception of, Aristotle's works. Consequently, his reading of Aristotle, although often historically plausible, is enriched by that of later pagan, Christian, and Arabic-language philosophical traditions. Aristotelian philosophy was in some ways an effort of many individuals who worked in different cultural and historical settings.

In his own work, Aquinas incorporates Aristotle's moral thought into what he thinks the Christian philosophical and theological tradition has accomplished. Even though the Bible, early Christian Fathers, and indeed other philosophical traditions determine or at least influence his wider outlook, in some way his approach is recognizably Aristotelian. For instance, the second part of Aquinas's unfinished three-part masterpiece, the *Summa Theologiae*, largely follows the order of the *Nicomachean Ethics*. This second part is itself divided into two parts (Torrell 2005, 17–48; Porro 2016, 281–304). In the first part of the second part, Aquinas first considers happiness, human action, and the virtues in general. Its topics include what is discussed in the *Nicomachean Ethics*, Books I–III.6. In the second part of the second part, Aquinas discusses the distinct virtues, and then the different states of life, such as the episcopacy, and the distinction between active and contemplative religious orders. The material on the virtues is divided between the cardinal virtues and the theological virtues. The section on the cardinal virtues includes but is not limited to most of the material treated in the *Nicomachean Ethics*, Books III.6–X.5. Aquinas's discussion of the different states of life, and in particular the active and contemplative, recalls Aristotle's comparison of the different kinds of happiness in Book X, 6–8. Overall, Aquinas's second part includes much of what is discussed in the *Nicomachean Ethics* and in generally the same order. But it brings in much else and only partially because it is enriched or expanded by accounts of specifically theological virtues, such as faith, hope, and charity, as well as theological concerns with sin, grace, and law.

Aquinas's moral philosophy is not simply that of Aristotle, or one among many versions of Aristotelianism. Aquinas's developed account of virtue draws also on such non-Aristotelian figures as Cicero and Macrobius and on Pseudo-Andronicus of Rhodes, who was perhaps an Aristotelian with heavy Stoic influences (Pinckaers 1992, 3–25). Aquinas incorporates them into a coherent whole that makes it difficult to extract the distinct strands upon which he works. Aquinas's concern is for truth rather than for originality or for a merely historically accurate account of his predecessors. Even though he does not aim for originality, his synthesis of such disparate strands gives rise to an original account that can put him at odds with other and subsequent members of the philosophical and religious traditions to which he belongs.

Aquinas shows a special interest in philosophical ethics, which he understands to be a particular branch of moral philosophy, which is a practical science. The practical sciences differ from the speculative sciences because they are about what humans can do. For instance, the movement of the stars is known by speculative science, but shipbuilding is a practical science. Moral philosophy differs from technical skills, such as shipbuilding or horsemanship, because it is about human actions themselves and not about what humans make. Technical skill is about what can be produced. Moral philosophy is about what can be done. Aquinas writes, "The subject of moral philosophy is human operation ordered to an end, or even a human being insofar as he is acting voluntarily for the sake of an end."[1] The end in this context corresponds to the Greek *telos* and is a goal for action. This difference between moral philosophy and technical skill can be seen in the different ends of a shipbuilder. By making a seaworthy ship, the shipbuilder exercises his skill. The end is the ship. By charging the just amount, he acts morally. The end is being a just and happy human. If he involuntarily makes defective ships, he fails with respect to shipbuilding. If he charges too much for even seaworthy ships, he acts unjustly and is a defective human.

---

[1] "Subiectum moralis philosophiae est operatio humana ordinata in finem vel etiam homo prout est voluntarie agens propter finem." *SLE*, lib. 1, lect. 1.

Aquinas understands "moral philosophy" to cover three distinct species of moral philosophy, or moral science.[2] Only one corresponds to what we would today count as ethics, which is the consideration of the good individual. The *Nicomachean Ethics* belongs to this branch of moral philosophy. The other two kinds of philosophy correspond to the other natural units of human life – namely, the household and the political community. Aristotle wrote distinct works about these parts of moral philosophy. Although Aquinas thinks that the human, the household, and the political community are studied by distinct kinds of moral philosophy, he also thinks that there is a necessary connection between them. In order to achieve one's own good, it is necessary to recognize that one is good in the context of a household and a political community. Nevertheless, he thinks that the *Nicomachean Ethics* belongs to its own kind of moral science – namely, that which is concerned with the individual, although it considers the individual in the wider context of the family and the political community. In this book we will follow contemporary usage of the term *moral* as applying primarily to the study of an individual's good, although it should be kept in mind that Aquinas thinks that this science of the individual's good belongs alongside the two other moral sciences.

Aquinas's use of *moral* also conflicts with commonly found attempts to account for moral obligation as only about duties to others and as entirely distinct or even divorced from other practical obligations. For Aquinas, moral philosophy is about what ultimately explains and justifies all human acts and practical reasoning – namely, the human end or good. It is not about a particular kind of action, such as shipbuilding, oratory, or even the rules of polite behavior. Moral philosophy considers what makes an act reasonable or not, which ultimately is about whether the human act is good and makes the agent good. No human act escapes moral evaluation.

This short work is about the central elements of Aquinas's moral philosophy, and not about his theology or more speculative parts of his thought. The purpose of this book is to explain how Aquinas understands the connection between three elements of human action. First, human acts are rationally justifiable and morally good because of their goal or end – namely, human happiness. Second, moral virtues are the qualities whereby this end is attained. They are "moral" virtues because they perfect the appetite, whereas the intellectual virtues perfect the intellect. They are "habits" in his technical terminology, although they are distinct from what we would ordinarily describe as habits. In this life such moral virtue is a necessary but not sufficient condition for happiness. Third, the moral virtues presuppose the intellectual virtue of prudence, which applies the rule of

---

[2] *SLE*, lib. 1, lect. 1.

reason to acts. Moral goodness principally belongs to good acts, insofar as they are measured by the rule of reason. The moral virtues exist to produce such acts. Without revelation, we can know only that a happy life is achieved through the exercise of such virtue. It should be clear now that it is impossible to address adequately Aquinas's presentation of this position without mentioning a variety of earlier thinkers, such as Aristotle, Cicero, and Augustine, as well as some theological claims.

2 Part One: Happiness, the Ultimate End

Aquinas largely agrees with what he takes to be Aristotle's account of ends, reasons, and action, even though he adds significant precision. There is a way in which the end is the most important moral feature. The end justifies, motivates, and even specifies good actions. The ultimate or final end is the most important motive for action, and in some way it justifies the most general principles of action. Like Aristotle, Aquinas holds that humans by nature have an end to which they are directed and concerning which they do not deliberate – namely, happiness. Ethics is about acting so as to achieve such happiness.

This focus on the agent's own happiness might seem egoistic or even hedonistic. Earlier utilitarians such as John Stuart Mill had a similar view of happiness's importance, but they were concerned with the greatest happiness of the greatest number of persons, and they were unclear about how to describe this happiness. More recent utilitarians and their compatriots generally set aside the very notion of happiness for that of preference-satisfaction. On the other hand, Kant and many of those influenced by him mostly separate moral obligation from happiness. But a misreading of Aquinas as an egoist or even as a hedonist would overlook key elements of his thought. Aquinas, like Aristotle and members of other premodern moral traditions such as Stoicism, connects happiness with the human good and not primarily with the subject's own feelings and individual desires. Moreover, philosophers such as Aristotle and Aquinas subordinate the individual's good to that of the political community and the way in which Christians think that happiness involves willing God's good more than one's own. Consequently, Aquinas's focus on human happiness does not entail egoism in the sense that someone must or should will his own good against or above any other good.

This first part will consider the way in which Aquinas understands happiness to be the human good. First, he thinks that everything is ordered to its own perfection, but most of all to the perfection of the universe and to God's own separate goodness. Second, he holds that humans become good by participating in such an order. In making these points Aquinas combines material from Aristotle, other philosophers, and Christian writers. He develops these sources in ways that can seem innovative, even though he does not explicitly depart from the essential elements of Aristotle's philosophy or the Christian tradition.

According to Aquinas, the end-directedness of humans is to some extent an instance of the end-directedness of all substances. Aquinas accepts Aristotle's account of final causality, according to which every agent or efficient cause acts for an end.[3] This final causality is found even in agents that lack reason, or consciousness, or even life. In these cases, the final cause is the end term of a natural process, as when a mammal grows to its proper size and does not continue to grow. According to Aquinas, such an end-directedness is needed to account for the difference between one kind of action and another. For example, water can cool hot metal, but fire applied to a pot of water will make the water itself hot. The difference between the two actions is in their ends – namely, the cold metal and the hot water. Aquinas and his contemporaries think that without such final causality there would be no regularity or intelligibility in nature. In a world that lacks final causality, water might melt iron and fire might freeze water. Many of Aquinas's statements about particular instances of natural causation are imprecise or even false. But the thesis that substances have capacities and ends for action was widely accepted in his time and has at least some intrinsic plausibility.

According to both Aristotle and Aquinas, there is some essential connection between the nature of the good and that of the final cause.[4] William Wallace writes that in this sense the end "is somehow a perfection or good attained through the process" (Wallace 1996, 17). The good can be described as the end insofar as the end itself is an object of a desire or an inclination. This notion of an end or good includes but is not limited to moral goodness. Since all substances have ends, all substances are inclined to some goods, even if such substances are not subject to moral evaluation. In this manner of speaking, heat is the good to which fire tends. As the good, it explains what the fire is achieving through acting on something else. According to Aquinas and Aristotle, heavy objects naturally tend toward the center of the earth as a place of rest. The earth's center is the end of the motion. A heavy object naturally moves toward the center of the earth when an obstacle to its motion is removed; it moves against its inclination when it is thrown upward. Such inclinations are toward ends or goods, and indicate that there is a kind of nonrational and nonmoral goodness.

Such nonmoral goodness is more easily seen in the inclinations and appetites of living substances. For instance, we might discuss the way in which nutrition,

---

[3] *SCG* 3.1–3; *ST* I-II, q. 1, art. 1. Wallace (1996), 15–18.   [4] *SCG* 3.16; *ST* I, q. 5, art. 4.

growth, and reproduction are abilities of plants to act for what is good for them. A tree has roots in order to draw minerals and water from the soil and leaves to carry out photosynthesis, which in turn allows it to grow and reproduce. It is bad for it to have leaves that fall off or roots that fail to convey water. We easily distinguish between trees that are doing very poorly, such as severely diseased trees, and those that are healthy and doing well. There is something wrong with such a plant when it does not act in a way that is appropriate to its species. Furthermore, under appropriate conditions we describe water, fertilizer, and sunlight as good for the plant insofar as they contribute to its perfection.

Animals not only share the basic inclinations of the plants for growth and reproduction, they also have conscious inclinations or appetites. Animals, including humans, desire goods or ends that they know in some way. A dog not only eats but desires and moves toward food, and it pursues a mate in heat. We can describe its food or mate as good or bad for it, depending on the contribution to its survival and reproduction. Similarly, it is good for a dolphin to hunt as part of a pod and for a deer to run from predators. Such activities result from inclinations that follow from the animal's perception of its environment. Generally, these inclinations direct the animal to the good that perfects it. For instance, it would be bad for a deer to run toward predators or for a whale to cast itself ashore.

As can be seen, for Aquinas the term *good* is the kind of term which has a variety of different and yet interrelated meanings (McInerny, 1997, 12–34). In the language of medieval scholasticism, it is an "analogous term." The world consists of many kinds of substances, each with its own distinct kind of goodness and badness, as well as good and bad activities. Moreover, other substances can be related to it in good or bad ways. For instance, smell is more important for a wolf than for an eagle, and the ability to dig is good for a mole and not for a dolphin. Aquinas thinks that the term *good* has a more robust content when applied to higher beings – namely, those with more unity, perfection, and, among bodily creatures, more complexity. For instance, water is a relatively simple substance that has an inclination to flow downward and to cool, but it does not have distinct parts that work together and form a unity. We can pour the water of one glass into two distinct glasses without qualitatively or substantially altering it. In contrast, a tree has roots, a trunk, branches, and leaves that cooperate for the good of the whole tree. We cannot easily divide it in the way that we divide water, although we might cut off a branch from one tree in order to graft it onto another. Some individual trees are obviously better than other members of their species in that they can flourish amid inclement weather or adverse soil conditions. Consequently, the inclinations of a tree are higher and more complex than are those of an inanimate substance such as water.

An animal such as a wolf or a dolphin has an even higher level of unity and complexity and a more complicated good. It is a subject of thought or desire. According to Aquinas, psychological predicates such as perceiving and desiring can be predicated of organs such as the eye but are most properly predicated of the whole living substance. The wolf or the dolphin is the primary subject of such activities. Although wolves hunt in packs and dolphins in pods, an individual dolphin or wolf is numerically distinct from another individual of the same species and has a correspondingly distinct set of desires and perceptions. One wolf might want the same food or mate that another wolf wants or be afraid of the same fire. He cooperates with other wolves by hunting in packs, but the packs do not have the same kind of unity that the individual wolf does. Similarly, the dolphin hunts as part of a pod, but the pod does not have the same kind of unity as the dolphin does. Different behaviors and objects are good or bad for the individual dolphin or wolf, both as an individual and in relation to the pod or pack and ultimately to the whole species. Dolphins, wolves, and other animals act to attain what they perceive as good for them and flee what they perceive as evil. Their natural inclinations and appetites mostly direct them toward their flourishing as individuals and as a species.

What connects the different meanings of goodness in the above cases? Different substances have different inclinations and ends. Aristotle and Aquinas connect goodness with function.[5] For instance, a good knife is sharp and a good hammer has a flat face. Similarly, being a good dolphin depends on swimming more than being a good wolf does. "Goodness" does not indicate just any quality or activity of a substance, but rather is relative to the proper functioning of the thing. For example, wolves and dolphins have a tendency to fall toward the earth, like water or stones. But we do not consider the goodness of a wolf or a dolphin to consist primarily in what it shares with stones.

This consideration of natural goodness sheds light on the goodness that is most relevant to moral philosophy, or what we might call "moral goodness." Humans intellectually apprehend the good and can consequently will it. The human good depends on what is proper to human nature – namely, reason. It involves acting reasonably, which is the function of the whole human being. We can consider separately the functions of organs, such as eyes and ears, or the function that humans might perform as part of the community, such as being a leather maker or a boat builder. But moral philosophy, or ethics, is primarily concerned with the function of the whole human being and not human parts or

---

[5] *NE*, I.7; *SLE*, lib. 1, lect. 9–11.

partial roles. Moral goodness is consequently a kind of goodness that is achieved when humans act in accordance with their inclination toward a good as part of or leading to the ultimate end. By nature humans are directed toward an ultimate end. By using reason humans act for the ultimate end.

Sometimes Christian ethics is thought of as merely about God or God's commands. Since Aquinas is primarily a moral theologian and not only a philosopher, we might be surprised at his emphasis on particularly human goodness. But following Aristotle, he rejects the Platonic emphasis on a separate "Form of the Good" in favor of what is properly human.[6] Even though both Aristotle and Aquinas agree that there is a separate good of the universe, they reject the Platonic account of its relevance for ordinary moral reasoning. They hold that the separate good is the immaterial Prime Mover, which is the final cause of the whole universe, existing separately from the universe in a way that a general exists apart from his army.[7] This separate good of the universe keeps everything in motion as one end of the universe. Nevertheless, its activity as a final cause does not take away from the intrinsic goodness that creatures possess, nor the different roles they play in the perfection of the universe. This separate good is sought by the immaterial beings that rule the universe as well as the apparently unconscious celestial spheres that move around the earth.

Even though Plato was incorrect in holding that knowledge of the separate Good is necessary and sufficient for yielding fully practical conclusions, he was perhaps correct to recognize its special place in moral philosophy. For both Aquinas and Aristotle, the immaterial Prime Mover, which is the separate good, is the ultimate end of both the universe and of particular humans. Consequently, it plays a central role in accounting for the human good. According to Aristotle, the Prime Mover seems to be important for ethics primarily because the best human life consists in contemplating it.[8] The last book of the *Nicomachean Ethics* dissatisfies many readers because Aristotle seems to exalt the intellectual virtue of the philosopher who contemplates the Prime Mover over ordinary moral virtues, such as justice and courage. He is unclear about the relationship between the happiness of the contemplative life and the moral life, and he seems unconcerned with conventional religious duties.

Aquinas and the preceding philosophical tradition identify Aristotle's Prime Mover with the God of the Jewish, Christian, and Muslim scriptures. Aquinas thinks that God and religion are central to moral philosophy. In this respect he differs from most post-Enlightenment philosophers and perhaps even from

---

[6] *NE* 1.6; *SLE*, lib. 1, lect. 6–8.   [7] *Met.* 12.10; *In Met.*, lib. 12, lec. 12; *ST* I, q. 6, art. 4.
[8] *NE* 10.7–8; *SLE*, lib. 10, lect. 10–13.

Aristotle. Aquinas's philosophical account of religion is not narrowly Christian, but draws largely on Cicero and Neoplatonic philosophers.[9] He particularly relies on Cicero's account of religion as the moral virtue whereby we render what we can to God. It is connected with justice, although it is its own distinct virtue, and it is in a sense the most important of the moral virtues. Moreover, Aquinas incorporates Neoplatonic accounts of moral virtue as a preparation for divine contemplation.[10] Following these pagan sources, Aquinas thinks that religion is a moral virtue, and that even nonreligious moral virtues are preparatory for contact with God.

In addition to using such pagan sources, he develops moral philosophy along lines that seem indicated by the Bible. For instance, he thinks that the command to love God is the most important and easily known moral obligation even apart from divine revelation.[11] In some contexts it can be difficult to know the extent to which Aquinas is practicing moral philosophy or moral theology. Particularly in the area of God and religion, Aquinas finds human nature to be not only morally insufficient but also corrupted by original sin. He thinks that the corrupted human nature that we know is not capable of living well without special revelation and help from God, especially with respect to the most important moral command to love God.[12] Nevertheless, it is plain to Aquinas that studying the moral virtue of religion and the natural obligation to love God more than self belongs to moral philosophy and not only to moral theology.

The Prime Mover, or God, plays an especially important role in Aquinas's account of the human ultimate end, which is the first principle of human action and consequently ethics (Pinckaers 2005, 93–114; Müller 2013). Aquinas develops Aristotle's scattered remarks at the beginning of the *Nicomachean Ethics* into an extended argument for the thesis that humans act for an ultimate end and that this ultimate end in some way is both happiness and God.[13] Although contemporary scholarly literature is divided over whether Aristotle means to argue for the existence of an ultimate end and, if so, whether the argument is valid, Aquinas provides an interpretation of the argument that is valid, although it may be, to some extent, formal and empty of content. It concludes to the existence of an ultimate end without stating immediately what that ultimate end is or the extent to which it is one or many.[14]

Aquinas develops this argument for the ultimate end in many texts. In the second part of the *Summa Theologiae*, Aquinas begins his account of

---

[9] *ST* II-II, q. 81.   [10] *ST* I-II, q. 61, art.5; *DV* q. 26, art. 8, ad 2.

[11] *ST* I-II, q. 100, art. 3, ad 1.   [12] *ST* I-II, q. 100, art. 5, ad 1; q. 109, art. 3–4.

[13] *ST* I-II, qq. 1–5. A much lengthier argument can be found in *SCG* 3.1–83.

[14] For its unity, see especially *ST* I-II, q. 1, art. 5, ad 1; art. 6, ad 1 and ad 2.

moral thought with an account of the end of human action and argues for the
position that all actions are for an ultimate end, which is in some way one. As
we have seen, acts are distinct from each other according to the ends to which
they are directed. Human acts are directed to ends that are known and willed
by the agent. For instance, an act of theft is different from an act of adultery
insofar as the agent knows and wills distinct ends. Aquinas, developing
Aristotle's text in the *Nicomachean Ethics* and perhaps more fully in book
II of the *Metaphysics*, argues that an intermediate end can be willed only on
account of some further end.[15] In the *Metaphysics*, Aristotle had argued that it
is impossible to proceed to infinity in what Aquinas would describe as an
essentially ordered series of causes, including the final cause. Since humans,
like other substances, are ordered to their own perfection and ultimately to
that of the whole universe as an ultimate end, the ultimate explanation of
human action must be the first principle of natural reasoning and human
willing – namely, human perfection as part of the whole. Consequently, any
particular end of action must be part of or subordinate to such a final end. In
this argument Aquinas and Aristotle make no claims about what the ultimate
end is. Aquinas, following Aristotle, establishes first only that it exists. In
later questions he considers its nature.

Aquinas's account of the ultimate end's nature draws together themes from
Aristotle and the Christian tradition. He notes that humans differ from other
animals through their ability to reason and choose a good that is understood on
the intellectual level; consequently, the human good consists in the peculiarly
human activity of acting in accordance with reason.[16] Substances that lack
consciousness are directed to ends merely by natural inclination. For instance,
a tree perfects itself by growing and reproducing. Other animals know their ends
through sense perception and are directed to them more or less by a natural
appetite. Wolves and dolphins are able to perceive what could contribute to their
good or what could harm them, and they are directed by their natural desires to
or against the perceived objects. In contrast, humans can think abstractly about
what their ends might be.

Unlike other animals, humans are free to act for apparent but not true goods
or for one of several true but incompatible goods.[17] The desire for pleasure
can cause someone to judge that something is good that is not, such as over-
indulgence in food or drink. Aquinas writes, "That which is apprehended as an

---

[15] *ST* I-II, q. 1, art. 4–7; *SLE*, lib. 1, lect. 2; *In Met.*, lib. 2, lect. 4. *NE* 1.2.1094a18-20; *Met.*
2.2.994b9-15.

[16] *SCG* 3.1, 17, 22–25; *ST* q. 1, art. 8.

[17] *In Sent.*, lib. 2, d. 25, q. 1, art. 1c; *DV* q. 24, art. 2; *DM* q. 6; *ST* I, q. 59, art. 3. See Gallagher
(1991).

apparent good cannot be entirely not good, but is good in a qualified way."[18] The food or drink itself is good, but consuming too much of it is not. In this case, the food is in some way good, even though it is not a true good for the agent. Sometimes the goods that are the objects of natural inclination can be incompatible with each other. A good object of natural inclinations can be evil in certain circumstances, and what would otherwise be evil can become good. For instance, generally it is bad for the agent to die. Someone should act so as to protect one's one life. On the other hand, preserving one's life might conflict with other goods, such as justice or temperance. For example, someone might order another to commit murder or adultery under the threat of death. Even though suicide is always wrong, it is better to undergo certain death at someone else's hands than to commit murder or adultery. Similarly, someone might act justly through holding political office or both justly and bravely through serving as a soldier. Both acts can be good, and yet a particular agent might be forced to choose between them. These choices are between goods that are all objects of natural inclination. Reason is needed to indicate which goods should be pursued and how they should be.

Human freedom to choose between different goods indicates an additional level of complexity in human happiness, in that even on a natural level there are various degrees and kinds of happiness. For instance, someone might choose not between good and evil but between a generally greater good and a lesser good. Aquinas thinks that such a case would be one of choosing a religious vow of chastity over marriage and reproduction. Moreover, human reason not only directs the way that the good is achieved but also has its own good – namely, truth. Consequently, there is in Aquinas as well as in Aristotle a distinction between a life of good political and moral action, which is happiness in an imperfect sense, and the more perfect life of contemplation. Such a variety of goods is unavailable to other animals since their perfection is more determinate because they lack reason.

This activity in accordance with reason is happiness, which is a good of the rational soul. In many ways Aquinas follows Aristotle's arguments against the positions that happiness is found in honor, money, or pleasure.[19] Like Aristotle, Aquinas starts with commonly held positions about happiness and indicates how they might both fall short and yet point to the truth. He devotes more attention than Aristotle does in the *Nicomachean Ethics* to the suggestion that happiness might consist in wealth. Aquinas himself appeals to Aristotle's *Politics* to argue that the desire for wealth is artificial and therefore limitless

---

[18] "Ilud quod apprehenditur ut apparens bonum non potest esse omnino non bonum sed secundum aliquid bonum est." *DV* q. 18, art. 6, ad 2. See also *DM* q. 11, art. 1c; q. 12, art. 2c.

[19] *ST* I-II, q. 2, art. 1–5.

in such a way that it cannot satisfy.[20] The purpose of money is to serve human nature, and not to subordinate human nature to lower material goods. Aquinas also develops an argument that happiness cannot consist in power over others. Power is a principle of human action and not properly an end for human action. It certainly could not be the final end. We would still need to know the end for which the power should be exercised. Power in itself can belong both to the good and the bad, and it can be used well or poorly. Consequently, although a happy human being would make good use of power, the happiness itself could never be in its mere possession. In general, external goods, such as wealth and power, are subject to loss by fortune in a way that seems incompatible with the human good, and they are themselves capable of bad use.

Similarly, happiness cannot consist in a good of the body, such as health or even in physical pleasure.[21] Aquinas develops Aristotle's account of happiness as rational activity by applying it to his own more sophisticated account of human nature, according to which humans have subsistent rational souls that not only are superior to the body but are capable of individual existence after death. Given the rational soul's superiority to the body, the human good must primarily belong to the soul and not to the body.

Like Aristotle, Aquinas thinks that pleasure accompanies or supervenes on activities when a power or ability acts on account of a suitable good (White 2013). For instance, different pleasures accompany eating and the reproductive act. Both Aquinas and Aristotle sharply distinguish between the pleasures that accompany rational activity and the pleasures that accompany merely bodily activity. The pleasures that accompany eating and reproduction are distinct from the higher pleasure of studying metaphysics. Consequently, pleasures differ in kind according to the way in which the actions differ – namely, on account of their power and ultimately their object or good. Aristotle and Aquinas do not merely recognize that some pleasures are superior to others. They make the stronger point that pleasures are willed, or perhaps should be willed, in conjunction with some good. Someone who acts for sexual pleasure is acting on the desire for sexual activity and not food. Similarly, someone who eats to satisfy hunger is acting on the desire for food and not for sexual activity.

Pleasure cannot be separated from the activity that it accompanies. We might try perversely to separate the pleasure from the end of the activity, especially in the context of bodily pleasures. However, in some cases it is difficult to know what that would mean. For instance, what would it mean to separate the pleasure of doing metaphysics from doing metaphysics or the pleasure of acting bravely from brave action? If someone were to claim to desire the pleasure of

---

[20] *Pol.* 1.9.   [21] *ST* I-II, q. 2, art. 5–6.

contemplating the First Cause without the actual contemplation, we might question the cogency of the desire or perhaps the truth of the assertion. If pleasure and action were separable, it might even be possible to make the pleasure that usually belongs to one activity accompany a quite different activity. In such a case, would it be possible for someone to desire the pleasure of bravery and not the pleasure of contemplating as an accompaniment to the act of contemplating? Aquinas thinks that to desire the pleasure of contemplation is in a way to desire contemplation itself, and similarly to desire the pleasure of acting bravely is in a way to desire to perform brave acts. The pleasures that belong to the different kinds of virtue are specifically distinct from each other and inseparable from their virtuous activities.

Aquinas, following both Aristotle and Augustine, states that pleasure always accompanies happiness, even though it plays no part in its definition.[22] If happiness consists of an activity of a power with respect to goods that are suitable to it, then happiness will be pleasurable. Happiness is pleasurable in the way that humans are capable of laughter – namely, on account of what it is and not because it is part of what it is. Humans essentially are rational animals. The ability to laugh is not part of this human essence, although it comes from it. The fact that humans are rational means that they can understand incongruities, and the fact that they have animal bodies make them able to laugh. Consequently, humans can laugh precisely because they are rational animals, even though the ability to laugh is not part of their definition. Similarly, happiness is pleasurable since it involves human powers and suitable goods. But the definition of happiness does not include pleasure.

In the *Nicomachean Ethics*, Aristotle identifies happiness with the ultimate end, and defines happiness as "an activity in accordance with perfect virtue."[23] Aquinas also holds that happiness is the ultimate end, but he more explicitly makes the further claim that God is the ultimate end.[24] He can hold both positions because of a distinction that he makes about the ultimate end. He thinks that in its most complete or perfect form, happiness is the heavenly contemplation of God and also that God is the separate good of the whole universe, including its human parts. His twofold description of the ultimate end depends on the distinction between the end considered as a thing in itself and the end considered as the possession or attainment of a thing. He explains this distinction through using the example of a miser and his money. We can consider the miser's one end in two ways. First, the end is the thing

---

[22] See also *ST* I-II, q. 4, art. 1. For Aristotle, see *NE* 1.8.1099a7-30; *SLE*, lib. 1, lect. 13.
[23] "Operatio secundum virtutem perfectam." *NE* 1.13.1102a5, quoted in *ST* I-II, q. 3, art. 2, sc.
[24] *ST* I-II, q. 2, art. 7.

itself – namely, the money. Second, the end is the miser's possession or attainment of the money. There are two distinct ways of speaking about the same end. Similarly, both God and happiness are the ultimate end of human action. If we consider the thing in itself, then we can say that God is the ultimate end. If we consider the end insofar as it is attained or possessed, then we can say that the ultimate end of human action is happiness.

Aquinas's account of perfect happiness as in some way the attainment or possession of God might seem to conflict with Aristotle's own account of happiness as the activity of apparently ordinary moral and intellectual virtue. Nevertheless, there is an obvious connection to Aristotle's description of perfect happiness as the contemplation of the Prime Mover in this life, as well as to the wider Aristotelian scheme whereby the Prime Mover is the final cause and separate good of the universe. Aquinas blends Aristotle's account of the Prime Mover and object of contemplation with a Christian account of God as the sole object that can satisfy the human intellect and will. This latter approach leads to the conclusion that God is happiness since "happiness is the perfect good that entirely quiets the appetite."[25] The human will is left unsatisfied with any particular goods since it is directed to the universal good, which is found only in God. Every created good is such only through participation in God's own goodness. Consequently, complete happiness lies only in knowing and loving God as he is in himself, which Christians think is possible only in the next life.[26]

Aquinas thinks that through revelation we know that a higher human happiness is possible because God makes us able to know him clearly and love him as the source of supernatural goods, which is the beatific vision. In his lectures on St. Matthew's Gospel, Aquinas even uses Augustine's *Commentary on the Sermon of the Mount* to argue that the beatitudes describe how happiness consists not in virtuous activity or even philosophical contemplation in this life but in the beatific vision of the next.[27] For instance, "Blessed are the poor in spirit" indicates that true happiness cannot be found in riches. The beatitudes address philosophical questions about the nature of happiness and to some extent correspond to pagan philosophical views. But Aristotle and other pagan philosophers were unable to know about perfect happiness since it exceeds the inclination of human nature and unaided human abilities. In the *Summa Theologiae*, Aquinas similarly uses the beatitudes in his description of

---

[25] "Beatitudo enim est bonum perfectum, quod totaliter quietat appetitum." *ST* I-II, q. 2, art. 8. For the argument, see also q. 3, art. 2.

[26] *ST* I, q. 12, art. 4; I-II, q. 3, art. 8; q. 5, art. 5.

[27] *Sup. Mat.,* lect. 5. See Pinckaers (2005), 104–106.

how happiness is attained not through the pursuit of pleasure but instead through the exercise of virtue and at last the heavenly vision of God.[28]

In general, Aquinas thinks that revelation supplements and corrects the works of moral philosophers. Moral philosophy is about that imperfect happiness which is attained through the purely human exercise of virtue in this life. Aquinas's moral theology is about attaining that perfect happiness of seeing God in heaven. Aquinas makes one of his rare criticisms of Aristotle in the previously mentioned discussion of beatitude in his lectures on St. Matthew. According to Aquinas, Aristotle erred by holding that perfect happiness can be attained through the contemplation of God through the exercise of intellectual virtue in this life. Aquinas notes that such knowledge can never completely satisfy our human nature.

If all actions are for the ultimate end, and the ultimate end is God, then how is moral error possible? Aquinas's account of happiness and the beatific vision sheds some light on the way in which happiness is related to human choice (McCluskey 2000). All human action is for happiness, but not all human action is directed to the beatific vision. His account of human freedom differs from that of later writers because he thinks that free choice is ultimately rooted in a natural – and consequently unfree – desire of the will for the agent's own happiness. Like Aristotle, Aquinas states that we will the end, happiness, by nature, and we deliberate merely about the means to or instances of this end. Aquinas concludes that because the will is ordered to the universal good and because God raises the natural inclination for happiness and fully satisfies it in the next life, the agent in the beatific vision lacks the freedom to will anything in opposition to God. However, lacking the vision of God in heaven, we can think of objects as good and choose them even if they are not good for us, all things being considered.

Free choice is possible because no good other than the universal good necessitates the will.[29] This choice can be between different particular goods or between real goods and merely apparent goods. For instance, someone might mistakenly think of theft or adultery as good, or at least of the property or the sexual activity as good. Both Aristotle and Aquinas think that theft and adultery are evil in every situation and consequently incompatible with happiness.[30] Nevertheless, we can think of them as good and choose accordingly. Consequently, for Aristotle and even for Aquinas, all moral disorder depends on ignorance or a false judgment concerning what is truly good for the agent.[31]

---

[28] *ST* I-II, q. 69. See Pinckaers (2005), 124–129.   [29] *ST* I, q. 82, art. 1–2; I-II, q. 10, art. 2.

[30] *NE* 2.6.1107a10-18; *SLE*, lib. 2, lect. 7. For Aquinas and his immediate predecessors, see Pinckaers (2005), 185–235.

[31] *NE* 3.1.1110b28-30; 7.3; *ST* I-II, q. 76, art. 4, ad 1; 77, art. 2c; *DV* 24, art. 8c.

The disordered agent, at least at the time of action, judges that the act is part of his happiness, or contributes to it, even if it does not. Insofar as freedom consists in the ability to sin, it depends on the ability to judge falsely about human action. Later theologians will argue not only that sin can occur without ignorance or positive intellectual error but also that the will is free to choose something apart from happiness or even reject happiness. On some such accounts, those who enjoy the beatific vision could will against it. These views are precursors to modern and contemporary notions of a free will that can choose any object, whether it is judged to be good or evil. Such an account is foreign to Aquinas, who thinks that every human act has a natural order to happiness.

It can be unclear whether Aquinas's discussion of happiness belongs to philosophy. Aquinas's distinction between perfect and imperfect happiness is not exhaustive, nor does it always bear the same signification; most especially, the distinction does not apply only to the distinction between happiness in this life and happiness in the next. For instance, in his *Commentary on the Nicomachean Ethics*, Aquinas first describes any happiness in this life as imperfect, but then describes the happiness of contemplation in this life as a perfect happiness in comparison with the exercise of moral virtue.[32] In his discussion of the beatitudes, Aquinas states that even in this life, holy persons have a beginning of heavenly happiness, even though such happiness is subordinated to the beatific vision of the next life.[33] Aquinas interprets the Christian beatitudes (*beatitudines*) as indicating such happiness (*beatitudo*). The imperfect happiness that is studied by philosophy is imperfect not only because it belongs to this life but also because it does not essentially require grace or revelation. Imperfect natural happiness does not necessarily require the possibility of the beatific vision, although it would seem to require some knowledge of God and the fulfillment of the command to love God. It is natural in the sense that it is proportionate to human abilities as God created them and not insofar as they are elevated in a special way by God. Aquinas and his contemporaries call such elevation "grace" because it is freely given by God to the nature that he creates. We might see supernatural happiness as a determination or special fulfillment of this natural happiness, although we should keep in mind that the human inclination to supernatural happiness is in itself added to human nature by God, and that the beatific vision exceeds the ability and inclination of unassisted human nature (Feingold 2004).

The imperfect natural happiness that belongs to this life can be achieved through action that perfects human nature. This description of happiness should

---

[32] *SLE*, lib. 1, lect. 10; lib. 10, lect. 11. See Müller (2013): 59–62, 70.
[33] *ST* I-II, q. 69, art. 2c; *Sup. Mat.*, lect. 5.

be understood in light of the distinction between the practical knowledge that is concerned with making or production and that which is about doing or acting.[34] Someone might act well and yet be bad at carpentry or farming. He would be a good human being although a bad carpenter or farmer. Similarly, the good carpenter or farmer might be a bad human being, in that he has failed precisely in being human and in reaching not only his supernatural but also his natural end. Generally speaking, creatures as a whole achieve their ends. Trees grow and reproduce, and dolphins swim and hunt. According to Aquinas, humans seem to be the only animals that largely fail to achieve their natural end. Aristotle, like many other ancient philosophers, noted that virtue is difficult and belongs only to the few.[35] Unlike Aristotle, Aquinas emphasizes that at least through grace, virtue and happiness are possible to all human beings.[36] Nevertheless, few humans overcome their desire for pleasure in this life or achieve the beatific vision in the next.[37] This failure to attain the end is not merely on account of the elevation of human nature to an ultimate end that exceeds human powers, but also through the disorders that are inherited as part of original sin. Because of such disorder, humans are unable to live even natural fully good lives without the healing grace that is infused at baptism alongside the specifically supernatural virtues and gifts.

In order to understand Aquinas's accounts of virtue and practical reasoning, it is necessary to keep in mind that humans by nature are inclined to perfection and that, more precisely, humans attain their perfection by directing their own actions. In Aquinas's *Summa Theologiae*, as well as in the *Nicomachean Ethics*, the consideration the ultimate end as happiness precedes and leads to is a systematic account of virtue. The human actions by which humans attain happiness are perfected and produced by such virtue. Consequently, Aquinas's account of human action, like that of Aristotle, demands a substantial account of what virtue is and how it is acquired. Even presumably apart from supernatural assistance, and certainly apart from revelation, philosophers such as Aristotle rightly saw that happiness depends upon the virtues and consists in their exercise.

3 Part Two: Virtue

In order to grasp Aquinas's account of the imperfect happiness in this life as virtuous activity, it is important to understand his definition or definitions of virtue and to consider what the different virtues are. These different virtues in

---

[34] *SLE*, lib. 2, lect. 4; lib. 6, lect. 4.   [35] *NE* 1.4.1095a22-23; 7.7.1150a15; 7.10.1152a25.
[36] *SLE*, lib. 1, lect. 14; *ST* I, q. 88, art. 1c.
[37] *ST* I, q. 63, art. 9, ad 1; II-II, q. 95, art. 5, ad 2; *DM* q. 1, art. 3, ad 17. See also *SLE*, lib. 7, lect. 7, 10.

general do not exist in isolation from each other but are connected. Aquinas thinks that a great number of specifically distinct virtues must be present for such happiness in this life and that different happy agents may need to emphasize different virtues. A consideration of the way in which the virtues cover the whole of the moral life will show how the good life requires the practice of all of the major moral virtues and that such virtue presupposes and is presupposed by correct moral reasoning. Moreover, Aquinas's account of justice indicates how his understanding of happiness as the end of human action does not entail egoism.

When Aristotle states that happiness is "activity in accordance with virtue," his notion of "virtue" does not carry the same moral overtones that it does for us today. In Aristotle's Greek, *virtue* (*arête*) indicates an excellence. In a wider sense, the same word can indicate those properties that make other animals good, such as a horse's speed. Moral philosophy is concerned with peculiarly human excellences or virtues, which include such obviously moral virtues as justice and courage but also other moral virtues, such as liberality and wit, as well as intellectual virtues, such as wisdom and knowledge. Aquinas uses the Latin word *virtus*, which, like the Greek word, has a wider application outside its use in moral philosophy. This Latin word sometimes refers to manliness, strength, and courage. In moral philosophy, it is used to translate the Greek *arête* as used not only by Aristotle but also by Plato, Socrates, and later Hellenistic philosophers, such as the Stoics.

As we have seen, although Aristotle thought that happiness was not virtue, he defined it as virtuous activity. The Stoics were particularly known for holding the stronger thesis that virtue is sufficient for happiness. For the Stoics, a virtuous person cannot fail to be happy. Even though early Christians were influenced by Stoic accounts of virtue, they strongly rejected this Stoic thesis. For instance, Augustine emphasizes the misery of the present life and the need for grace. Nevertheless, Stoic descriptions of the virtues, especially in the form passed on by Cicero's *De Officiis*, provide much of the framework in which Aquinas and his medieval contemporaries work. Aquinas inherited a philosophical notion of virtue as central to moral philosophy and necessarily connected with happiness.

Several definitions of virtue can be found in Aristotle's works. For example, after connecting happiness with virtue in book I of the *Nicomachean Ethics*, Aristotle defines moral virtue in book II as "an elective habit consisting in a mean relative to us, determined by reason, as the wise human being will determine it."[38] In another passage he describes virtue more broadly as that

---

[38] "habitus electivus in medietate consistens determinata ratione, prout sapiens determinabit." *NE* 2.6.1106b36-1107a2, as cited by Aquinas in *ST* I-II, q. 59, art. 1c.

"which makes the one having it good and renders his act good."[39] Among the many later definitions of virtue, the most important is that which Peter Lombard develops from the works of Augustine, according to which virtue is a "good quality of the mind, by which we live rightly, which no one uses badly, which God works in us without us."[40] In the *Summa Theologiae*, Aquinas seems to think that this Augustinian definition is compatible with the Aristotelian account.[41] For example, since Aristotle thinks that habit belongs to the category of quality, Aquinas holds that the "quality of mind" indicated by the Augustinian definition is in fact a habit. Aquinas himself defends the thesis that virtue is a "good operative habit." This last definition also applies to all the different virtues, including both the moral and the intellectual virtues that Aristotle lists, as well as the centrally important Christian virtues that were recognized by the scholastic tradition – namely, faith, hope, and charity.

For Aquinas, the words *habit* and *operative* have a precise philosophical meaning. In his Aristotelian metaphysics, any created being is either a substance, which is more or less something that exists on its own, or an accident, which is a being that exists immediately or ultimately in a substance. For instance, a pig is a substance, whereas its shape and color are accidents that inhere in the pig. Habit is a fairly broad genus, which Aquinas, following Aristotle, defines as "'a disposition according to which a thing is disposed well or badly, either according to itself,' that is, according to its nature, 'or in relation to another,' that is, in order to its end."[42] A habit is a quality that inheres in a substance or in other accidents that inhere in a substance. It is not concerned with the substance's mere existence, but rather with how it exists well or badly. For instance, a human body is capable of existing in different ways. The habits of sickness and health are those habits or dispositions by which the body functions well or badly. Similarly, beauty and ugliness are bodily habits or dispositions.

In Aquinas's Aristotelian terminology, an operative habit such as a virtue is not precisely what we might think of as a "habit" in English, which could include mere animal conditioning or a physical addiction.[43] It is a particular kind of habit that belongs to intellectual substances. Operative habits are principles of operations, which are acts of intellectual substances. These

---

[39] "bonum facit habentem, et opus eius bonum reddit." *NE* 1106a16, cited in *ST* I-II, q. 55, art. 2, sc.

[40] "bona qualitas mentis, qua recte vivitur, qua nullus male utitur, quam Deus in nobis sine nobis operatur." Aquinas, *ST* I-II, q. 55, art. 4, obj. 1.

[41] *ST* I-II, q. 55, art. 4.

[42] "'dispositio secundum quam bene vel male disponitur dispositum aut secundum se,' idest secundum suam naturam, 'aut ad aliud,' idest in ordine ad finem." Aquinas, *ST* I-II, q. 49, art. 3. The quoted text is from *Met.* 5.20.1022b10-11.

[43] *ST* I-II, q. 50, art. 3, ad 2; q. 55, art. 2, ad 2.

operative habits do not cause acts on their own, but they cause the acts to be performed promptly, pleasurably, and consistently. Humans need such habits because, unlike other animals and merely natural substances, they lack a determinate order to one end or goal. For instance, a rock falls merely by being a rock, a tree similarly grows, and deer flee predators. But humans can choose between different ultimate ends, such as pleasure, wealth, and honor. Moreover, different humans achieve excellence through different and often incompatible activities, such as warfare, large public expenditures, and political activity. The habits that produce the relevant human acts must exist in the reason or in the faculties that are subordinate to reason. An animal that lacks reason, such as a deer or a lion, cannot have an operative habit.

There is a way in which humans, like other animals, can be influenced to act in certain ways by bodily conditions. Both Aristotle and Aquinas recognize that these bodily qualities are not strictly speaking virtues, even though they can influence human acts. Aristotle and Aquinas describe these qualities as "natural virtues" by which humans are directed toward one operation on account of their individual bodily natures.[44] They are not habits or virtues in the strict sense. On account of such "natural virtues," someone who is naturally mild mannered will be unlikely to become overly angry, and someone who is naturally courageous will be unlikely to submit to excessive fear. These bodily features influence human action, even though they are not rooted in reason or in other powers that participate in reason.

Since these "natural virtues," like the qualities of other animals, are directed to one operation and are independent of reason, they cannot consistently cause virtuous actions. For example, the naturally "courageous" person resembles a lion.[45] A lion's acts are metaphorically courageous or cruel. The naturally courageous person will be inclined to those kinds of acts, which if chosen would be the kinds of acts that are performed by the courageous or cruel person. Consequently, a human's merely natural "courage" inclines the agent to the cruel act in the same way that it inclines to the courageous act. In contrast, true virtues perfect the properly human powers of intellect and will and those powers that in some way need to come under their influence. A fully courageous person follows the order of reason and consequently is not cruel.

Apart from their connection with reason, nonrational human powers do not need virtues. For instance, the power of sight does not require a habit in order to see, and the power of hearing does not require a habit in order to hear. They are directed to one kind of operation. Some nonrational powers, such as that which makes anger possible, need virtues to moderate them. Virtues assist powers that

---

[44] *NE* 6.13; *SLE*, lib. 6, lect. 11; *ST* I-II, q. 63, art. 1; *DVC*, art. 8.   [45] *DVC*, art. 8, ad 10

can be ordered in different ways. Since humans have intellect and will, properly human acts are not determinate by the natural virtues and dispositions, even though they can be influenced by them. The operative habits differ from merely natural "virtues" in that they help to produce particularly human acts, which proceed from the intellect and the will. They are like nature to the extent that they help to produce one kind of act, but they are unlike nature in that they produce human acts. For this reason, Aquinas follows the earlier tradition in his use of the phrase "custom is another nature."[46] In order for the intellect and will to act in a consistent way, similar to the way that nature acts, they must be modified by operative habits.

An operative habit is a kind of habit, and a virtue is a kind of operative habit. Like nonoperative habits, such as health or sickness, operative habits can be either good or bad. For example, the good operative habit of temperance is a principle of good human actions that perfect the agent, whereas the bad operative habit of intemperance is a principle of bad human actions that make the agent bad. Virtue is a good operative habit, and vice is a bad operative habit.[47] A virtuous person performs good acts firmly, promptly, and pleasurably.[48] Such good acts constitute and lead to the ultimate end, which is human happiness. A vicious person is inclined to the opposed acts. For instance, the virtue of temperance inclines the agent to eat a moderate amount in a moderate way, and the virtue of intemperance inclines to immoderate eating.

Virtue perfects the agent by inhering in the agent's intellect and will or in those powers that are subordinate to reason. These latter powers are not like the power of sight or of moving, which immediately follow reason unless there is some sort of defect or impediment. The nonrational powers that can be perfected by virtue are subject to reason according to what Aquinas, following Aristotle, describes as a constitutional or royal manner as opposed to a despotic one.[49] Those under despotic rule have no ability to resist the ruler's commands. In contrast, those under a constitutional or royal rule retain something by which they can resist. According to Aquinas, the appetitive power is divided into the will, which is an appetite that follows reason and is intrinsically rational, and the sense appetites, which follow sensation. The sense appetites undergo what Aquinas calls "passions," which are like emotions in that they are felt experiences that follow on the perception of some good or evil that we perceive sensibly. Unlike the rational appetite or will, the

---

[46] "consuetudo est altera natura." *DVC*, art. 8, ad 16; art. 9c.; *DV*, q. 24, art. 10c.

[47] *ST* I-II, q. 55, art. 3; q. 71, art. 1.   [48] *DVC*, art. 1, ad 13; *DVCarit.*, art. 2c.

[49] *ST* I, q. 81, art. 3, ad 2; I-II, q. 17, art. 7. Jensen (2013): 203–208; Lombardo (2018): 122–123. Aquinas refers to Aristotle, *Pol.* 1.5.1254b2-5.

sense appetites are not intrinsically rational. Nevertheless, they participate in reason in that they can be ruled by it indirectly. Although the sense appetites seem to be the most commonly discussed instances of nonrational subjects of virtue, they are not the only such powers. For instance, the cogitative power is a cognitive sense power that works with the intellect in its thinking about particular good and bad objects. It can be perfected by virtue because it participates in reason

These powers that follow reason constitutionally or politically require moral virtue because they do not immediately follow the intellect and the will in the way that other bodily movements can. A human can usually directly choose whether or not to pick up a cup or walk across a room. Bodily movements can be trained, but merely physical training does not lead to a habit as understood by Aristotle or Aquinas. For instance, someone through physical exercise might develop the muscles and skills to wield effectively a weapon in battle. Such training might in some way involve virtue, but it need not. In themselves, the muscles and nervous system do not participate in reason, even though they obey it. The arm wields the weapon in simple obedience to reason. In contrast, the ability to undergo emotions, what Aquinas describes as the "sense appetites," does not immediately come under reason. Humans often cannot choose to become immediately angry, sad, or joyful. Nevertheless, these sense appetites can be changed in such a way that they assist in the production of good action so that the agent becomes angry, sad, or joyful in the right way and at the right time. They do not obey reason in the way that a slave obeys a master, but they participate in it. Consequently, these sense appetites can be the subjects of virtue. But since they are to some extent independent of reason, they are not by themselves distinctively human powers. Many animals who lack reason possess these powers. The presence of such powers makes it possible for these animals to possess the previously mentioned "natural virtue," as in the case of a lion's inclination to acts that can in some way be described as courageous. But, as we have seen, such natural virtue strictly speaking is not virtue.

Aquinas's account of virtue as a good operative habit allows him to more precisely describe the way in which happiness is a virtuous activity and to connect Aristotle's account of virtue with that of the Christian tradition. Like Augustine, he rejects the Stoic thesis that virtue is sufficient for happiness. He also thinks that Aristotle rejected a version of this claim that predated Stoicism.[50] Unlike Aristotle and perhaps even unlike Augustine, Aquinas provides a more developed metaphysical reason for this rejection.

---

[50] *NE* 1.7.1098a3-5; *SLE*, lib. 1, lect. 10; *ST* I-II, q. 3, art. 2.

Aquinas thinks that operations make possible a likeness to God. In the *Summa Theologiae*'s discussion of happiness, he notes that everything is perfect insofar as it is in act and not merely insofar as it is in potency to act. A substance becomes perfect not through a mere ability or potency to act well but by acting well. The ultimate act for humans is not just the act of being human but an operation performed by a human. Consequently, the ultimate end of human life considered as something attained by the agent – namely, happiness – is an operation. Later in the same work, Aquinas develops the way in which such an operation makes the agent more like God. He writes, "Since the substance of God is his action, the highest assimilation to God is according to some operation ... The felicity or happiness by which a human being is conformed to God, which is the end of human life, consists in operation."[51] In these arguments Aquinas incorporates into a metaphysical and even somewhat theological framework the definition of virtue as an operative habit and the claim that happiness itself is an operation.

There is no real distinction between a life of virtuous action and the happy life or good life. The agent's goodness is produced by or perhaps consists in good operations. For this reason, virtues make the agent good. Vices are bad operative habits that make the agent bad. For instance, a habitual thief steals consistently, promptly, and pleasurably. The habit may make him a good thief, but he will be a bad human being.[52] A good thief is "good" only metaphorically. In contrast to the vices, virtues make someone good, and moral virtues make someone good as a human being. The goodness of the operations is prior to the goodness of the virtues because the goodness of the habit comes from the fact that it produces good acts, and the agent's happiness consist in or depends on such acts. A virtuous person is the same as a good person. Consequently, Aquinas's ethics can be described as a virtue ethics to the extent that the subject matter of moral philosophy – namely, the imperfect human happiness attainable naturally in this life – is the matter of some acquired moral virtue.

Different notions or aspects of happiness are connected with different kinds of virtue. First, like Aristotle, Aquinas distinguishes between moral and intellectual virtue. Aquinas's moral philosophy, as opposed to his moral theology, is primarily concerned with the moral virtues that follow the rule of reason and are acquired by human acts, as well as the associated virtue of prudence. The moral virtues are distinguished from mechanical, or technical skills, and intellectual virtues.[53] Technical skills, such as building or farming, are habits, but they

---

[51] "cum Dei substantia sit eius actio, summa assimilatio hominis ad Deum est secundum aliquam operationem ... felicitas sive beatitudo, per quam homo maxime Deo conformatur, quae est finis humanae vitae, in operatione consistit." *ST* I-II,q. 55, art. 2, ad 3.

[52] *ST* I-II, q. 55, art. 3, ad 1. See *Met.* 5.16.1021b17; *In Met.*, lib. 5, lect. 18.   [53] *ST* I-II, q. 58.

produce good products rather than good human actions or agents. Intellectual virtues, such as mathematics or natural philosophy, make the agent good insofar as they perfect the intellect. Consequently, in themselves they are higher than the moral virtues. But since they do not on their own make the agent good, they are in a way inferior to the moral virtues. Prudence is unusual since, although it is an intellectual virtue, it depends on and is necessary for moral virtue.

The definition of virtue as a "good operative habit" allows Aquinas to give a more philosophically defensible account of Lombard's Augustinian definition of virtue.[54] According to Aquinas, this traditional definition is in terms of the Aristotelian four causes – namely, the formal, the material, the final, and the efficient. A formal cause makes something what it is. The formal cause of virtue is the genus, in this case an operative habit, and its specific difference, which is the habit's goodness. The definition of *virtue* as a good operative habit indicates the form. For Aquinas it is unproblematic that Lombard's definition mentions "quality" rather than "habit" because according to Aristotle a habit belongs to the genus of quality. The material cause more or less is what something is made of. Lombard's definition refers to the matter that is the subject of virtue – namely, the mind. As we have seen, Aquinas thinks that virtue resides in the powers of the soul that are either themselves rational or in some way rational by participation. The final cause is the purpose, end, or goal. The end of virtue is its operation, which Lombard's traditional definition indicates in its account of virtue as "by which we live rightly, which no one uses badly."

The efficient cause provides some difficulty for Aquinas's appropriation of Lombard's definition. An efficient cause is the agent that brings about the act. According to Aquinas, Lombard's definition identifies the efficient cause with God in the part that reads, "which God works in us without us." Aquinas does not apply this part of the definition to an Aristotelian definition of virtue. The Christian thinkers who preceded Aquinas developed a distinction between the traditional moral virtues that are discussed by philosophers and the theological virtues, which exceed human abilities and are directly about God (Bejcvy 1990). Influenced by this tradition, Aquinas distinguishes between virtues that are described by the philosophers and those that are known and acquired through divine help. Aquinas holds that this part of the definition applies only to those Christian virtues that are caused directly by God and are described as "infused virtues." Since they exceed natural powers, they cannot be acquired; their acts cannot be performed without divine help.

These virtues cannot be acquired through merely human effort.[55] The virtues that are infused directly by God are the theological ones of faith, hope, and

---

[54] *ST* I, q. 55, art. 4; *DVC*, art. 2.   [55] *ST* I-II, qq. 62–63.

charity, or infused moral virtues that help the agent to attain supernatural happiness. These infused moral virtues perfect humans with respect to their ultimate supernatural end and follow a different supernatural role than that of their corresponding acquired moral virtues. Moral philosophy as practiced by Aristotle, Cicero, and even by moral theologians such as Aquinas, is concerned with the acquired virtues that in some way perfect humans and not immediately with such infused virtues.

Our concern is primarily with Aquinas's moral philosophy and consequently with his account of acquired moral virtue. However, when Aquinas discusses particular moral virtues and prudence, it can be difficult to know whether he has in mind the acquired, the infused, or both indistinctly. Two reasons for this difficulty are that he draws on both the Christian tradition and pagan philosophers in his account of the virtues and that he organizes them around the four cardinal virtues of prudence, temperance, courage, and justice (Bejcvy 2007). Plato was among the first to emphasize these four virtues, and they are listed together in the Book of Wisdom, which may have been influenced by Hellenistic philosophy. Ambrose of Milan may have been the first to call these four virtues cardinal, from the Latin word for "hinge" (*cardo*). These four virtues are like the hinge upon which the well-lived life turns. Aquinas notes that although prudence is an intellectual virtue, it can be numbered among the moral virtues because of this role.[56]

In order to understand Aquinas's account of virtue, it is important to grasp the way in which he organizes the different virtues around the four cardinal virtues. This schema allows us to see his understanding of the virtuous life in greater detail. Aquinas himself considers the cardinal virtues in two ways, as distinct formalities that are present in the same act and as specifically distinct habits.[57] First, reflecting an earlier medieval and scholastic tradition, cardinal virtues are all formalities, or general conditions, of each virtuous act.[58] The "formality" in this context seems to indicate an essential characteristic of the act or the way that it is done. For instance, every virtuous act will be prudent in its consideration of reason, just in the rightness of the exterior operation, temperate in its restraint of inordinate passion, and courageous in its firmness against such passion.

Second, and more properly speaking, the cardinal virtues are specifically distinct habits that differ from each other and from other virtues. Their acts are specifically distinct from the acts of other virtues. Considered in this way, each cardinal virtue is about a different kind of object. In scholastic terminology, it

---

[56] *ST* I-II, q. 58, art. 3, ad 1. For the connection with moral virtue, see q. 57, art. 4.
[57] *ST* I-II, q. 61, art. 3–4; *DVC*, art. 12, ad 23.
[58] Lottin (1949), 142–46; Houser (2002), 305–309.

has its own subject matter and formal object. For instance, temperance is about restraint in food and drink, and courage is about reasonably facing death in battle or martyrdom. They are principal virtues because of the way in which they exemplify certain characteristic features. In contrast to some of his earlier scholastic predecessors, Aquinas primarily thinks of a cardinal virtue in this way – namely, as a specifically distinct habit and not as a formality. But remnants of the earlier use are spread throughout his work. At the end of this section, it will be seen that even though Aquinas thinks that there are many specifically distinct virtuous habits that operate independently, almost all of the moral virtues are needed in some way in order to live happily. Their variety and number show that the good life requires many different kinds of action and can be instantiated in many different ways.

Before considering the connection of the moral virtues, it is important to look at the way in which Aquinas takes into account a great number of distinct moral virtues. Unlike Aristotle, Aquinas uses the four cardinal virtues as the organizational principle in his taxonomy of the different moral virtues and consequently his treatment of the moral life as a whole. The first part of the second part of the *Summa Theologiae* introduces the virtues and provides a general account of moral principles, including virtue. Its account of virtue is philosophically rich, but it does not allow us to deduce much about Aquinas's understanding of particular good lives. Fortunately, the second part of the second part is much lengthier and devoted entirely to a discussion of more concrete moral questions. It is organized largely around the various virtues. He seems to have written it as a better-organized alternative to the standard textbooks that were then in use (Boyle 2002, 9–12).

In this second part of the second part, Aquinas is concerned with particular actions rather than more universal truths because he is guiding those who will preach and hear confessions. He divides his account of particular actions into a treatment of the virtues, supernatural gifts, and opposed vices and a study of the different states of life and their duties. His discussion of the virtues covers the general subject matter of morals. Aquinas treats the moral virtues at length after he gives his account of the three theological virtues. Although his description of the moral virtues is in a theological context, he draws on and develops philosophical material. The theological concern for particular cases perhaps causes him to consider the moral virtues in much greater detail than his philosophical sources did. In this case theology seems to stimulate moral philosophy.

Aquinas's taxonomy of the virtues is an essential, somewhat original, but also now neglected aspect of his theory of virtue, perhaps because of its length and complexity. It is significant in that he uses it as a guide for evaluating particular actions, and consequently it provides us with a more concrete picture of what he regards as the happy life of virtuous action. Its broad outlines are helpful for illustrating the connection between happiness and the virtuous life, even though in this work much material must be summarized. Moreover, the description of the cardinal virtues, and in particular the virtues that are associated with prudence, will allow us to grasp the relationship between virtue and moral rules.

Although the *Summa Theologiae* is theological, Aquinas's schema of the moral virtues is an intelligent reworking of earlier schemas that were developed by three pagan writers – namely, Cicero, who was influenced on this point by Stoics; the Neoplatonist Macrobius; and the author of the *De virtutibus et vitiis* portion of the *Peri patheon*, Pseudo-Andronicus of Rhodes, who seems to have been an Aristotelian with Stoic influences.[59] Aquinas's description of any particular moral virtue often rests primarily on Aristotle or on one of these other authors. Nevertheless, as has been mentioned, he is focused not only on acquired virtue but also on the infused virtues that share the same matter. For instance, his discussion of temperance covers fasting not only as a Christian duty but also as part of the natural law.[60] They both are concerned with the same subject matter – namely, abstaining from food. Aquinas often does not indicate whether he is concerned primarily with the acquired or the infused virtues.

In the schema of the second part of the second part, all the moral virtues are in some way reduced to the cardinal virtues as parts of them. Aquinas associates other moral virtues with the cardinal virtues by describing them as integral, subjective, and potential parts of the virtues.[61] This distinction would have been easily understood by his first readers but does not clearly correspond to any contemporary description of parts. The first two parts – namely, the integral and subjective, are more obviously parts in a sense that we would recognize. Integral parts make up a whole but can be separated from it. For instance, the walls and the foundation are integral parts of a house. Subjective parts are complete wholes that are members of a species or genus. For instance, the species "lion" and "cow" are subjective parts of the genus "animal." Potential parts typically are parts only through the way in which some power or potency is part of the whole to which it belongs, as the sense and digestive powers or potencies are parts of the animal soul. The soul has them as parts, even though it is not made of them in the way that the body is made of different integral parts, such as the digestive organs and the eyes.

---

[59] For the *De virtutibus et vitiis*, see Cacouros 2003, 528–530, 545–546,

[60] *ST* II-II, q. 147, art. 3.

[61] *ST* II-II, q. 48, art. un. My summary of the particular virtues is indebted to Goudin (1680): 408–456.

A cardinal virtue has all three kinds of part. It can be made up of other virtues that are integral parts, or it can be a genus that has different species under it. In addition, it has potential parts of a virtue more loosely connected to it, as somehow sharing in its characteristics. Aquinas's use of the different kinds of parts allows him to organize all of the moral virtues around the four cardinal virtues, including the distinct virtues that were treated not only by Aristotle but also by his later sources. The virtues that they describe are all parts of a cardinal virtue in one of the three ways. Again, we can see how Aquinas incorporates different traditions into his own overarching framework.

Aquinas discusses the cardinal virtues in an order different from that in which they are treated in the *Nicomachean Ethics*. Whereas Aristotle discusses prudence only after the moral virtues, Aquinas discusses it first among the cardinal virtues, immediately following his account of the theological virtues. Strictly speaking, prudence is "right reason about action."[62] More narrowly, the proper act of prudence is to command right action.[63] Aquinas's emphasis on this act of command partly distinguishes prudence from the technical skills, which like prudence are also practical intellectual habits. One difference between prudence and technical skill illustrates the way in which prudence is fully practical. Since prudence helps the agent's intellect to command right action, it cannot be used incorrectly. In contrast, technical skill helps its possessor to know how to make to make a good product or bring about a good result. The skilled agent judges correctly but can use the skill to bring about the opposite result. For instance, a good carpenter knows not only how to make a sturdy chair but also a chair that fails at the right time. If he voluntarily makes such a defective chair on purpose as part of a practical joke, the chair's defect does not indicate that he lacks skill. Similarly, a physician who on purpose kills someone by administering poison will probably be more skillful than a physician who accidentally kills a patient. The faulty chair and the dead patient do not on their own indicate a lack of skill. In contrast, bad acts indicate a lack of prudence. Someone who knows what is right to do but fails to command the act fails precisely by being imprudent.

Aquinas states that the cardinal virtue of prudence has fifteen virtues as parts.[64] There are eight integral parts, four subjective parts, and three potential parts. Aquinas thinks that the integral parts all fit together as necessary conditions of the one virtue of prudence. These different parts come not only from Aristotle but from his other sources. They are related to prudence in the way that

---

[62] "recta ratio agibilium." Among many passages, see especially *ST* I-II, q. 57, art. 4c; q. 58, art. 4–5. See *NE* 6.5.

[63] *ST* II-II, q. 47, art. 8. See *NE* 6.5.1140b22-25, 6.10.1143a8.   [64] *ST* II-II, q. 48, art. un.

walls and a roof are related to the house. Consequently, even if Aristotle did not discuss each of them, he discusses the prudence of which they are parts. Similarly, we might imagine someone discussing a house without talking about its roofs or walls explicitly. We might be able to incorporate her description of the house with our own and someone else's account of the description of its parts.

The integral parts of prudence are each needed either for knowing a particular action or for ordering it.[65] Five integral parts are concerned with knowing the particular good action. According to Aquinas, the only integral part of prudence that Aristotle discusses is "solertia," which is a quickness of thought. The virtue of reason (*ratio*) is an ability to apply general principles to a particular action, and the virtue of understanding (*intellectus*) is not what Aristotle calls "understanding" – namely, an insight into principles – but instead an insight into the particular action. Docility (*docilitas*) is the ability to take into account another's advice. Aquinas finds each of these three virtues in Macrobius. He finds another integral part in Cicero – namely, memory (*memoria*), which is not a power of the soul but instead an acquired ability to draw on past experiences when judging an action.

The three other integral parts of prudence are about ordering an action. Aquinas finds them all in Macrobius. Foresight (*providentia*) takes into account what needs to be done in light of the future, circumspection (*circumspectio*) is an attention to all relevant present circumstances, and carefulness (*cautio*) considers possible bad effects and dangers. Aquinas uses Macrobius and Cicero not to correct Aristotle but to add to the more broadly Aristotelian account. He is concerned with our knowledge of the virtue that is described by Aristotle and not merely with Aristotle's own words about it. It seems to me that Aristotle, if given the opportunity, might have recognized that prudence must include these virtues that are described by later authors.

The integral parts of prudence make up prudence.[66] In contrast, the subjective parts are themselves in some way complete instances of prudence, even though they are about different subject matters. These subjective parts of prudence correspond to the three natural unities that individuate the different moral sciences – namely, the individual, the household, and the political community. The individual and the household each have their own prudence. Both political prudence and military prudence are about the political community. Political prudence is about its internal order, and military prudence is about resisting external threats. Unlike the integral parts of prudence, they are each fully a habit of prudence. But they are parts to the extent that they produce right reason

---

[65] *ST* II-II, q. 49.   [66] *ST* II-II, q. 50.

within a partial moral sphere and not the whole of human action. Aquinas
stresses that these kinds of prudence are distinct habits because they are about
different objects. They are acquired and used differently. But they are related to
each other in a way comparable to how the different moral sciences are
connected, in that they are all about human action and the good of a naturally
occurring human individual or group.

Aquinas takes the three potential parts of prudence directly from the
Nicomachean Ethics, and even keeps the Greek name of each virtue.[67] These
potential parts do not issue commands but are about the intellectual acts that are
needed for them. After grasping the end to which it is ordered by moral virtue,
the prudent reason must be able to deliberate about different ways of achieving
this end. Aristotle states that the virtue of "eubulia" perfects such deliberation.
In contrast, the virtues of "synesis" and "gnome" perfect right judgment,
although in different ways. "Synesis" is correctness in judging according to
normal rules of reasoning, such as that one ought to return what has been
borrowed. "Gnome" covers the exceptions to such rules, as when what has
been borrowed will be seriously misused if returned. These two virtues are to
some extent like the mechanical skills and unlike prudence because they issue
judgments. But they differ from mechanical skills in that they indicate what
actions should be commanded by prudence.

This discussion of the fifteen parts of prudence gives at least a flavor of how
Aquinas approaches particular morals. He is concerned with classifying different acts according to the different matter and incorporating what a variety of
earlier writers have written. He indicates that there are particular situations that
will require exceptions to normal rules, as is seen in his distinction between
gnome and *synesis*. He thinks that right reason requires a wide variety of habits
to fully operate, as is seen in his description of the many integral parts.
Moreover, he is concerned with the variety of different goods that are the
objects of reason – namely, the individual, the family, and the household. But
he does not discuss at length any one particular means, or provide any algo-
rithms, for arriving at the correct solution. Like his own contemporaries, and
unlike ours, Aquinas rarely if ever develops any stories or examples to illustrate
his use of principles. His discussion of particular morals is meant to provide
a framework in which we can recognize what is needed for a good action and
what can go wrong in a bad one.

Aquinas's account of prudence shows how the agent's reason should be
perfected. It is a description of an agent's good moral reasoning rather than an
abstract treatise on moral philosophy. Similarly, his account of the properly

---

[67] *NE* 6.9–11; *ST* II-II, q. 51.

moral virtues helps us to recognize what good human actions are about. Whereas prudence is concerned with right reason about the moral life as a whole, each moral virtue is concerned with one of its parts. We can use the framework of the cardinal and associated virtues in our judgment of particular actions.

Aquinas thinks that the three remaining cardinal virtues perfect the three kinds of human appetite.[68] The first division in human appetites is between the will and the sense appetite. Although the agent is free to choose between the apparent and the real good, or between different goods, he needs virtue to act well consistently, pleasurably, and firmly. Some virtues are necessary to regulate the disordered sense appetites that can conflict with reason. These are powers that are only rational by participation. For instance, the desire for too much cake might conflict with the judgment that too much cake is bad, or the fear of death in battle might cause a soldier to run away. The virtues of temperance and courage moderate such sense appetites so that they do not interfere with reason. Virtue is also needed to perfect the agent's will when she wills a good other than her own. This power is essentially rational. The will provides no obstacle to the agent's willing her own good. Justice regulates the willing of another's good.

According to Aquinas, the virtue of justice makes it possible for us to be happy through willing not our own good but that of another. It also situates us correctly in relation to other individuals and to the political community. This emphasis on justice helps to show how his focus on the agent's happiness is not egoistic. Justice is primarily about "right" (*ius*). In Latin there is a close connection between this word and the word for justice (*iustitia*).[69] The Latin "ius" in some contexts indicates a civil or ecclesiastical law, and in others it can mean the prerogative of a parent or ruler to exercise some authority, or even in some writers what we would call an individual's "right." Aquinas is primarily concerned with right insofar as it is an object of action or virtue. He writes that right is "some work adequate to another according to some mode of equality."[70] An instance of such right would be the amount of change that a cashier should give a customer or the amount of work that should be done for a wage. This right can be determined by reason or by human law, whether civil or ecclesiastical.

Aquinas includes the notion of right in his definition of justice as a "habit according to which someone by constant and perpetual will gives to everyone

---

[68] *ST* I-II, q. 61, art. 2; *DVCard.*, art. 1.

[69] *ST* II-II, q. 57. For the different significations, see art. 1, ad 1. For scholarly disagreement over Aquinas's account, see McInerny (1992), 207–219; Finnis (1998), 132–140.

[70] "aliquod opus adaequatum alteri secundum aliquem aequalitatis modum." *ST* II-II, q. 57, art. 2c.

his right."[71] He thinks that the elements of this definition correspond to what Aristotle describes as the three general requirements for an act to be virtuous – namely, that it be done knowingly, by choice for a right end, and from a firm character. Since justice is the cardinal virtue that belongs to the will, it is voluntary, and as voluntary it presupposes knowledge. The constancy and perpetuity of the will indicate its firmness.

Aquinas takes the three subjective parts of justice from Aristotle – namely, legal justice, commutative justice, and distributive justice.[72] But he more clearly explains how they correspond to the ordering between individuals and the community as well as that between individuals. Legal justice in its wider sense, which is also called general justice, is the species or subjective part of justice by which the citizen is ordered to the community.[73] Aquinas approvingly quotes Aristotle's statement that this general justice is "the most beautiful of the virtues, and neither Hesperus (The Evening Star) nor Lucifer (The Morning Star) is so admirable."[74] Justice in this widest sense is preeminent in that it commands the other virtues. For instance, general justice might command a citizen to face death bravely in defense of the common good. This virtue directs other virtues to a political common good that is greater than the individual's own good. The agent's happiness can only be achieved in the subordination of his own good to that of the wider community.

The two other subjective parts of justice govern two other relationships – namely, that of the political community to the citizen and that of one citizen to another.[75] Commutative justice considers this later relationship and especially equality in exchanges between individuals. Aquinas provides an especially lengthy account of vices that are opposed to commutative justice.[76] For instance, charging too much for an item or refusing the correct change is a violation of commutative justice. But it applies more widely to contracts, robbery, fraud, usury, murder and mutilation, as well as to the punishment of sins by a proper authority. It considers these interactions not insofar as they are governed by the supernatural charity but insofar as everyone receives her due. Aquinas, like other medieval writers, emphasizes that commutative justice covers not only works but also speech, such as insults and backbiting. His discussion of this virtue and sins against it provides an overall picture of how

---

[71] "habitus secundum quem aliquis constanti et perpetua voluntate ius suum unicuique tribuit." *ST* II-II, q. 58, art. 1c.

[72] *NE* 5.1–2.   [73] *ST* II-II, q. 58, art. 5.

[74] "praeclarissima virtutum videtur esse iustitia, et neque est Hesperus neque Lucifer ita admirabilis." EN 5.1.1129b27-28, quoted in *ST* II-II, q. 58, art. 12c.

[75] *ST* II-II, q. 58, art. 7–8.   [76] *ST* II-II, qq. 64–78.

humans should treat each other according to rules of equality. It is important that Aquinas does not reduce all of morality or even justice to such rules. They are an important part of the virtue of justice. But neither the rules of equality nor any other set of rules are sufficient for recognizing or determining all moral action.

Distributive justice covers the order of the political community to the individual. It is usually carried out by political authorities who have the role of distributing honors, awards, and commonly held material goods. The notion of equality in distributive justice is more complex than that of commutative justice. Aquinas follows Aristotle's account of the way in which distributive justice is about geometric equality and commutative justice about arithmetic equality. In commutative justice, the equality is determined by what is exchanged and not by the person. If someone sells a shoe to another, the relevant factors are the value of the shoe and what is paid for it. Personal qualities are irrelevant. This equality is arithmetic. In contrast, according to distributive justice, the authority should consider both what is distributed and the worth of the person to whom it is distributed. For instance, one person through courage in battle or political service may deserve a medal, or someone who sacrifices his own property to help the community might deserve reimbursement more than another does.

The relationship between the individual and the political community is undermined if one kind of justice is neglected or reduced to another kind. Happiness requires all three. If the specific distinction between these kinds of justice were passed over, we would be left with a seriously deficient view of the moral agent and consequently the good life (Pieper 1966: 70–75). In Aquinas's ethics, the good person cannot be considered entirely apart from the political community. If all justice were commutative justice, then what the individual owes the community would be seen as a kind of equal exchange. But there is no equality between the individual and the community of which he is naturally a part. How would someone be able to pay the community for his upbringing? What kind of material good or even honor would need to be given to justify self-sacrifice in battle? Thinking of the political community as a separate individual or group of individuals would make legal justice unthinkable. Moreover, if there were no distinct political authority, there would be no difference between just punishments and revenge. Aquinas follows the mainstream tradition by interpreting the Gospel command to avoid revenge as not a command to forego justice but rather a reminder that justice belongs to a proper authority, such as a ruler, and not to private persons.[77]

---

[77] *ST* II-II, q. 108, art. 1, ad 1.

Furthermore, Aquinas also thinks that justice must also consider individuals in relation to another and not just in relation to the political community. Focusing solely on the relationship between the citizen and the community, and consequently undermining the role of the individual, would destroy commutative justice, which presupposes that private citizens can have a strict equality when they exchange goods or services. The wider political community must recognize the somewhat independent relationships between its members. Misconceptions about the relationship between the citizen and the community threaten the very possibility of a part or parts of justice and consequently that of a virtuous and therefore happy life. Individual happiness can only be achieved through relationships with other individuals and with the political community. No single moral rule or virtue can determine how one should behave in such different contexts.

Some related virtues even involve a kind of right or due that is itself impossible to determine according to a rule. These potential parts of justice involve an aspect of equality or interaction with each other, but they lack the strict equality that we find in commutative justice and even in distributive justice. Some of these virtues are more important than justice or its parts because they involve debts that cannot be repaid. For instance, by piety we return to our parents some measure of what we have received from them, but what we give will never equal the life that has been given to us and our upbringing.[78] We can give someone a just amount of money for a pair of shoes, but we cannot give our parents such an amount. Similarly, what we owe in worship to God through the virtue of religion cannot be measured. This virtue of religion is in some way more important than justice because what we owe God is greater than what we owe to any individual or to the political community.[79]

Aquinas's emphasis on the cardinal virtues in his taxonomy of the virtues might give us a false picture of the good or happy life since we might be inclined to think of these cardinal virtues as more important than other virtues. The superiority of religion to justice illustrates how for Aquinas the cardinal virtues are not the most important virtues. As was mentioned above, a virtue is cardinal because it exemplifies certain principal features. For instance, justice is a cardinal virtue because of the equality that is part of its definition. Religion is not a cardinal virtue because it falls short of such equality. But on account of this same inequality, it is more important.

Up to this point, we have primarily discussed cardinal virtues that inhere in rational powers – namely, prudence, which is in the intellect, and justice, which

---

[78] *ST* II-II, q. 101.   [79] *ST* II-II, q. 81, art. 6.

is in the will. The reader might have the impression that Aquinas is uninterested in our emotions. But two cardinal virtues, courage and temperance, regulate our ability to experience such emotions. They are directed to another's good mostly through other virtues, such as justice. Aquinas describes these emotions as "passions" of the sense appetite (Lombardo 2018). The passions are psychosomatic responses to goods that are perceived by the senses. Although they involve the body, they are not essentially specified by the bodily changes. Their objects are about these perceived goods and evils. For example, an angry person might undergo certain bodily changes, such as an increase in heart rate, but anger is not about the heart rate but about a perceived injury. Virtues that regulate the passions are not as important as prudence or justice, but they are necessary for living well. Consequently, narrowly focusing on Aquinas's account of prudence and justice would give a somewhat misleading view of the way that the good life involves more than just the intellect and will.

Aquinas distinguishes between two kinds of sense appetite – namely, the concupiscible and the irascible.[80] The concupiscible appetite is simply about goods that are apprehended by the senses, such as food, drink, and sexual pleasure. Irascible appetites are about such goods insofar as they involve some difficulty, as when someone fears hunger or hopes for sexual pleasure. These sense appetites are shared with other animals. For instance, a dog might love bones and be moved by a desire for a bone much in the same way that a human can love and be moved by his desire for a beer. In humans, the desire can be regulated by the virtue of temperance. Similarly, a dog might wish to flee when attacked by a larger dog in much the same way that a soldier might wish to flee in battle. In humans, the cardinal virtue of courage can regulate this appetite.

Although Aristotle thinks that courage is about death in battle, Aquinas follows both pagan and Christian sources in applying the notion widely to include such as acts as undergoing martyrdom and in stating that there are connected secondary parts that are concerned with lesser dangers.[81] Aquinas also uses it as a way of incorporating Aristotle's account of magnanimity, which some scholars think is a kind of self-exaltation that is incompatible with Christian humility.[82] He finds the connection between magnanimity and courage in the somewhat Aristotelian Pseudo-Andronicus of Rhodes and follows some Stoic accounts of magnanimity as a virtue whereby someone is able to take on difficult tasks. According to Aquinas, magnanimity is not opposed to

---

[80] *ST* I, q. 81, art. 2. [81] *ST* II-II, q. 123, art. 4–5; q. 128, art. un. See Herdt (2013).
[82] *ST* II-II, q. 129, art. 2–4. Hoffmann (2008).

humility, but rather to pusillanimity in the face of danger.[83] Someone who lacks
magnanimity is afraid to act virtuously when it is difficult. Such magnanimity is
a potential part of courage because it is concerned with a difficult good –
namely, great virtue.

The cardinal virtue of temperance modifies the most typical of the
concupiscible appetites – namely, the desire for bodily pleasures and primarily the pleasure of taste.[84] Aquinas, like Aristotle, thinks that such pleasures
accompany good activities. But our desires for them need moderation because
we are inclined in the wrong way or to the wrong extent. The four subjective
parts of temperance are about different pleasures – namely, those of food,
drink, reproductive activity, and activities that are connected with reproductive activity.[85]

By itself, temperance is the least important cardinal virtue, although like the
others it is necessary for a virtuous life.[86] But two potential parts of temperance
are among the most significant moral virtues – namely, mildness and humility.
Like temperance, these two virtues restrain desires.[87] But unlike temperance,
neither of them are about bodily pleasure. Mildness restrains inordinate anger,
and is discussed at some length by Aristotle.[88] Aquinas departs from Aristotle
by connecting it with temperance. He states that mildness has a special
excellence because of the way in which it prevents anger from causing false
judgments.[89] Humility restrains the desire to excel.[90]

Aquinas's account of humility is rooted not only in Christianity but also in the
De virtutibus of the partially Aristotelian Pseudo-Andronicus. Aristotle does
not discuss humility at any length, although he does criticize boasting and
vanity.[91] According to Aquinas, Aristotle does not mention humility because
he is concerned primarily with political virtues.[92] Humility is about subjection.
The subjection to another that comes under civil law belongs to legal justice and
not to temperance. In contrast, humility is primarily about one's insignificance
before God.[93] Although humility primarily concerns subjection to God, it has
effects on one's dealings with other humans. For instance, we know that the evil
in us is from ourselves and that the good is from God, and we can recognize
God's goodness in our neighbor. This virtue of humility helps us act in a way
appropriate to this knowledge.

Like religion, humility is an instance of a moral virtue that is more important
than the cardinal virtue with which it is associated. Humility preserves the order
of reason in the agent's relation to God and whatever belongs to God in her

---

[83] *ST* II-II, q. 133, art. 2.   [84] *ST* II-II, q. 141, art. 4–5.   [85] *ST* II-II, q. 143, art. un.
[86] *ST* II-II, q. 141, art. 8.   [87] *ST* II-II, q. 161, art. 4.   [88] *NE* 4.5; *ST* II-II, q. 157, art. 1–2.
[89] *ST* II-II, q. 157, art. 4.   [90] *ST* II-II, q. 161, art. 1.   [91] *NE* 4.3.1125a28-33; 4.7.
[92] *ST* II-II, q. 161, art. 1, ad 5.   [93] *ST* II-II, q. 161, art. 3.

neighbor. This order is more important than that which is preserved by temperance, which belongs to the concupiscible appetite. After legal justice, which is the virtue most generally concerned with establishing the order of reason among persons, the most significant moral virtue is humility.[94]

This brief overview of the moral virtues indicates what Aquinas thinks human happiness consists in, especially the imperfect happiness of this life that is the activity of acquired moral virtue. He discusses the moral life in the context of the objects of the different moral virtues. Aquinas notes that these moral virtues are to some extent inseparable from each other. For instance, he does not think that someone can lead a happy life because of temperance and an unhappy one because of his injustice. Although no one moral algorithm completely regulates the way in which the virtues work with each other, he does think that they all without conflict contribute to one happy life. They must all be present.

It is important to distinguish between Aquinas's Aristotelian account of the connection between the virtues from the Stoic account of the unity of the virtues, which influences various Church Fathers. Like some of his medieval predecessors, Aquinas thinks that the cardinal virtues could be considered as present in every act if considered as formalities. But he is more concerned with the way in which distinct operative habits are connected to and with prudence. Aristotle's account of this connection was only recently made available to Aquinas and his contemporaries in the newly translated book VI of the *Nicomachean Ethics* (Lottin 1949, 197–252).

Like Aristotle, Aquinas thinks that each virtue can be acquired and exercised separately. Moderate acts of eating and drinking produce temperance, and reasonably facing death in battle produces courage.[95] Nevertheless, the virtues of everyday life are connected in such a way that someone who has one will have the others or at least be near to having them if given the opportunity.[96] For instance, a poor person will be unable to acquire magnificence or even liberality, which are the virtues for giving money.[97] But the liberal person will possess and practice magnanimity if given the opportunity. Aristotle and Aquinas argue that the moral virtues are connected with each other through prudence in such a way that a virtuous person will need to practice all the relevant moral virtues and will lack any vices.

Each moral virtue, including all of the cardinal virtues, requires the virtue of prudence, and prudence in turn depends on moral virtue.[98] As a source of correct thinking, it requires correct judgment and commands about its acts.

---

[94] *ST* II-II, q. 161, art. 5.   [95] *ST* I-II, q. 51, art. 2–3; q. 63, art. 2.

[96] *ST* I-II, q. 65, art. 1; *DVCard.*, art. 2.   [97] *ST* I-II, q. 65, art. 1, ad 1.

[98] *NE* 6.13; *SLE*, lib. 6, lect. 11; *ST* I-II, q. 58, art. 4–5.

Prudence itself is fully practical and consequently depends on moral virtue to direct it to the right end as well as its choice of the means. Therefore, not only does moral virtue depend on prudence, but prudence depends on moral virtue. The moral virtues are connected with each other through prudence because the agent cannot be prudent in one area, such as the matter of justice, and not in another, such as the matter of temperance.[99] The one virtue of prudence is concerned with the matter of all the moral virtues. For instance, a prudent person might need to decide between incompatible actions that involve different virtues, such as giving one's meager savings to feed one's parents or to pay a debt or to support the Church. Similarly, a prudent person will need courage to command a just action when such an action endangers her life or temperance to command a just action when tempted by bodily pleasure to avoid it. Like Aristotle, Aquinas thinks that intemperance destroys prudence.[100]

Aquinas's account of the moral virtues fills in the picture of what he thinks is the ultimate end of the moral virtues that are considered by the philosophers – namely, an imperfect happiness that is attainable in this life. Such happiness primarily involves the practice of justice, which governs social relations, as well as associated virtues such as piety and religion. But Aquinas is also concerned with temperance and courage, which regulate the agent's emotions and are directed primarily to the agent's own good. Although these virtues are subordinate to justice, they are necessary for living well.

Aquinas's description of the moral virtues on its own might seem lengthy and complicated, even considered apart from his wider account of the theological virtues, the gifts of the Holy Spirit, and the different states of life. But the multiplicity of the moral virtues sheds light on the multiple ways in which humans, unlike other animals, can flourish. Although every human has one ultimate end, the achievement of this end, at least insofar as it is naturally attained in this life, does not consist in any one kind of activity. Every good human life involves the practice of many connected but nevertheless specifically distinct human virtues. Moreover, good human lives will differ from each other in their exercise of such distinct virtues. All the relevant virtues must be practiced, even though they might not be practiced in the same way and to the same extent. Aquinas refuses to reduce the moral life to simple formulas or to a short list of moral traits and passions.

---

[99] *ST* I-II, q. 65, art. 1, ad 3–4.
[100] *NE* 6.5.1140b13-20; *SLE*, lib. 6, lect. 4; *ST* II-II, q. 53, art. 6; q. 153, art. 5.

Aquinas's account of the moral virtues raises two questions about his understanding of moral reasoning. First, is there any one principle that should govern all moral thinking, such as the principle of utility or the categorical imperative? His account of the moral life as a whole is organized according to the various virtues that were catalogued by his predecessors and does not seem to yield any universal formula for deciding right action. Second, if prudence depends on virtue, to what extent are agents who lack virtue capable of moral reasoning? Presumably vicious persons can make correct judgments. These two questions lead to a consideration of Aquinas's account of moral rules and their use.

4 Part Three: Moral Rules

Aquinas's account of moral reasoning covers both the purely practical reasoning of every human agent and the qualifiedly practical reasoning of the moral philosopher. As was shown in the previous part, there is a necessary interdependence between prudence, which is the intellectual virtue that perfects moral reasoning, and moral virtue. The proper act of prudence is the intellect's command of an act. It follows the will's choice of a means toward the end that is set by moral virtue. Even though prudence is intellectual, it presupposes moral rectitude and leads to action. In contrast to prudence, moral philosophy might be practical only in the sense that it is about human action or, perhaps more completely, insofar as it is concerned with the manner in which this action is done. Someone might know moral philosophy and yet fail to act virtuously.

Moral rules play a role not only in Aquinas's moral philosophy but also in his account of ordinary moral reasoning. In this respect, Aquinas differs from many contemporary virtue ethicists. But he agrees with many contemporary virtue ethicists in declining to base his moral philosophy or his account of moral reasoning on formal rules. He thinks that the use of such rules is necessary but insufficient for reasoning about human action for two reasons. First, practical reason is concerned with singular actions, whereas such moral rules are universal. Second, the agent's correct reasoning about singular actions largely depends on moral rectitude, whereas the grasp of some primary moral rules does not.

The ordinary knowledge of moral rules is not philosophical knowledge. Except insofar as they appeal to revealed truth, Aquinas's own writings on moral reasoning belong either to moral philosophy itself or to moral philosophy insofar as it has been adopted by or changed into moral theology. Although his moral philosophy is not fully practical, it is about fully practical acts and fully practical moral reasoning. This part will focus primarily on Aquinas's description of the ordinary agent's practical reasoning and not on

Aquinas's more general account of moral philosophy and its use of demonstration. These two kinds of moral reasoning – namely, the individual's fully practical reasoning and argumentation in moral philosophy – can be considered distinctly, even though they influence each other.

Moral reasoning uses principles about ends and statements about particular means that are brought under the end. For instance, a just person will be ordered to justice in such a way that he will at the proper time think that it is good to return borrowed items. This principle about returning borrowed items, combined with the recognition that the just person has a borrowed item to return, leads to the judgment and ultimately to the command that this borrowed item should be returned. According to Aquinas, although the correct most general principles are often unused, they are easily known to everyone, and other moral rules are derived from these principles. Insofar as both sets of principles are discoverable by human reason, they are the "natural law." The agent reaches the ultimate end, which is happiness, by using these principles (McInerny 1997, 35–59).

Although in contemporary moral theory Aquinas is sometimes described as a natural law theorist, he rarely uses the term *natural law* in his own writings. But he does frequently discuss those principles that can be described as the natural law. They are different ways of directing action toward the human good. The sinner either fails to follow a true practical judgement or follows a false one. Whereas theology considers such sin as an offense against God, moral philosophy considers it precisely insofar as the sin is against reason.[101]

According to St. Paul, the Gentiles, even though they lack the Mosaic law, have another law "written in their heart."[102] Christians identified this law written in the heart with the Stoic account of a law that follows human nature and ultimately is based on the reasonable order of the universe. Aquinas identifies this same natural law with the principles of practical reason that are knowable apart from revelation and are described by Aristotle as universal premises of a practical syllogism. Aquinas writes:

> And since practical reason also uses in some degree a syllogism in what can be done ... according to what the Philosopher teaches in Book VII of the *Ethics*, therefore we find in practical reason that which is related to operations in the same way as the proposition in speculative reason is to conclusions. And these sorts of universal propositions of practical reason, which are ordered to actions, have the nature of law.[103]

---

[101] *ST* I-II, q. 71, art. 6, ad 5.

[102] "scriptum in cordibus suis." Rom 2:15, in *ST* I-II, q. 106, art. 1, obj. 2; *Sup. Rom.*, cap. 7, lect. 4. See also *Sup. Rom.*, cap. 2, lect. 3.

[103] "Et quia ratio etiam practica utitur quodam syllogismo in operabilibus, ut supra habitum est, secundum quod philosophus docet in VII Ethic.; ideo est invenire aliquid in ratione practica quod ita se habeat ad operationes, sicut se habet propositio in ratione speculativa ad

These propositions are laws insofar as they regulate human action. They are principles because they are about universal acts. The prudent agent must apply them appropriately in a given set of circumstances.

Aquinas primarily uses the term *natural law* in his early *Commentary on the Sentences* and more systematically in the *Summa Theologiae*, I-II, qq. 90–108, which has been called the "Treatise on Law." It is often in whole or in part translated and published separately. Even in this treatise, natural law plays a relatively small part. Of its eighteen questions devoted to law, only one (q. 94) is primarily about the natural law. The other significant laws are the eternal law, which is God's Providence, human law, the Old or Mosaic law, and the New Law of the Gospel, which is grace. As is suitable for a theological work, Aquinas devotes much more attention to the last two, which together are called the divine law, than the other kinds of law. The treatment of the natural law seems to be preparatory for the later discussion of the divine law. But it is a necessary preparation, since the divine law presupposes the natural law. Moreover, this discussion of natural law is significant because it provides a context for Aquinas to develop central points about our knowledge and use of the universal principles of practical reason.

According to Aquinas, the notion of law has four characteristics.[104] First, law belongs to reason and not to the will since reason is what regulates and orders acts. Second, law must be ordered to the common good. A supposed law that is directed to the ruler's private good can be called "law" only in a derivative sense. Third, law must come from an authority. For instance, private citizens cannot make human laws that bind other private citizens, even if the laws are reasonable. Fourth, law must be promulgated. It cannot regulate acts if the agents cannot know it. Although these four characteristics are most clearly seen in human law, Aquinas thinks that they apply in some way to all law. For example, the whole universe is governed by God's eternal law.[105] Such orderly governance belongs to reason, is directed to the common good, and rests on God's own authority. The eternal law's promulgation seems more difficult to grasp. Aquinas notes that the eternal law is eternally written in the Divine Word – namely, the Second Person of the Trinity, and in the Book of Life, which lists the elect. It seems that we know about this promulgation through revelation rather than through philosophy.

The eternal law itself belongs to the definition of natural law, which is the rational creature's participation in the eternal law.[106] Remember that according

---

conclusiones. Et huiusmodi propositiones universales rationis practicae ordinatae ad actiones, habent rationem legis." *ST* I, q. 90, art. 1, ad 2.

[104] *ST* I-II, q. 90.   [105] *ST* I-II, q. 91, art. 1.   [106] *ST* I-II, q. 91, art. 2.

to Aquinas goodness is relative to a nature's proper function. Nonrational creatures have natures that are directed to one determinate good or end. For instance, fire heats and oak trees grow leaves. They do not choose how to attain their ends. For all Aristotelians, the regularity of such actions indicates their final cause. For Aquinas at least, this natural finality is part of the eternal law, which is God's intelligent ordering of the universe.[107] Substances that lack cognition act for ends that they do not know. Animals that have only sense cognition act only for the particular ends that they know through sensation and to which they are directed by the sense appetites, such as eating and reproduction. But rational animals can grasp with their intellects the end to which they are directed by nature. Humans can reason about the best means to or instance of this end. As we have seen, such means or instances are undetermined. Humans can choose between different true goods or even between true goods and what is merely apparently good. The natural law is the set of general practical precepts that guides humans in their good actions.

The difference between humans and other animals indicates the unique way in which humans participate in the eternal law.[108] Dolphins and wolves can act for the good in their own way without deliberating or using general principles. They are capable of comparing and determining in a limited way the best means to an end, such as hunting fish or moose, but they do not think abstractly about what is good for dolphins and wolves. In contrast, human actions, even though they are themselves singular, are governed by universal reason. For instance, when seeking food humans understand in some way that food is good for them and that their search for food can be limited by universal principles concerning other parts of the human good, such as those involving justice or religion. To follow the natural law is simply to act in accordance with the principles of reason.

These principles regulate the attainment of goods that are objects of natural inclination (Jensen 2015, 44–60). Following the Roman jurist Ulpian, Aquinas thinks that there are three relevant kinds of natural inclination.[109] First, by nature substances tend to remain in existence. Water on its own remains water unless it is destroyed through a chemical reaction. On a higher level, plants and animals fight disease and consume food that preserves life. Aquinas thinks that humans by natural inclination not only tend to their own existence but also recognize intellectually that such continued existence is good. Consequently, there are principles of the natural law that regulate the preservation of human life.

---

[107] *ST* I-II, q. 93.   [108] For a contemporary account, see MacIntyre (1999), 33–61.
[109] *ST* I-II, q. 94, art. 2c.

The second kind of inclination is that of animals for the preservation of the species, which is achieved through the reproduction and the education of their young. It is important to recognize that he is not saying that all animals do this in the same way. For instance, fish, deer, and wolves all reproduce and educate in different ways. Humans should reproduce and educate through the institution of the family, which consequently involves the recognition of special natural-law precepts that govern reproduction and the relationships between family members. For instance, it would be bad for humans to abandon their babies in the way that some fish do or to bring up their children in the family structures of wolves or deer.

The third kind of human inclination is not shared with other animals since it is directed to that which is proper to reason, which by nature is ordered to the truth about God and just relations with other humans in society. Consequently, humans have natural-law principles that help them to achieve these ends, such as the precepts against lying or blaspheming God. All natural-law precepts belong to reason, but these and related precepts are about goods to which our rational powers are inclined by their nature.

The human good in general, considered as happiness and even the attainment of God, in some way includes or presupposes these goods that are the objects of natural inclination (Jensen 2015, 61–84). The natural law indicates how to attain these goods. Consequently, the activity in which happiness consists – namely, activity in accordance with virtue – is the same as activity that is in accord with the natural law. There is no conflict between Aquinas's account of natural law and his emphasis on virtue. The acquired moral virtues are attained and practiced precisely through following those precepts of the natural reason that can also be described as the "natural law."

Humans are inclined to virtuous acts in much the same way that fire is inclined to make something hot.[110] But humans, unlike nonrational creatures, choose whether to act according to their inclinations and consequently for the human good. Every act of virtue belongs to the natural law because the human good is achieved through virtuous acts, and natural law is the set of universal propositions that are used in attaining this good. Aquinas thinks that virtuous acts require knowledge not only of singular goods but also of the more general goods that include them. Consequently, virtuous action requires the knowledge of some moral principles. Furthermore, the use of moral principles at least leads to the kinds of acts that virtue performs. An agent who consistently follows the natural law will eventually acquire the moral virtues.

---

[110] *ST* I-II, q. 94, art. 3.

These universal propositions of practical reason can be divided into affirmative and negative precepts.[111] Affirmative precepts, such as to honor one's parents or to help the needy, command acts of virtue.[112] These precepts always bind the agent, even though they do not bind the agent in all times and places (*semper sed non ad semper*). An agent is always held to honor his parents, but at any given time, the agent might be bound to do something else, such as to rescue a child from a well or to face death for one's political community. Sins against these precepts are often sins of omission that might not bind the individual to a particular time or place. For instance, the natural law requires one to worship God, but apart from further divine law, it does not say whether such worship should be given on a particular day, such as a Saturday or a Sunday. Similarly, honoring one's parents can often be moved ahead or behind an hour without any violation of the corresponding precept.

Negative precepts bind agents at all times and in all places. Such precepts include "Do not commit adultery" and "Do not dishonor one's parents." Although they bind always everywhere and at every time (*semper et ad semper*), they do not need to be used everywhere and at every time. For instance, an ordinary person might go a week without thinking of or using the precepts against murder and theft simply because she is doing other tasks. Violations of these negative precepts are generally acts of commission. For example, the negative precept to avoid dishonoring one's parents is violated by means of an act at a determinate time and place.

These negative moral principles exclude acts that would be incompatible with a virtuous life. Such acts are often described as "intrinsically evil" and include, among other acts, the three acts that Aristotle mentions should never be done – namely, murder, adultery, and theft.[113] There can be vagueness concerning what falls under the descriptions of such acts. For instance, an act of killing someone could be an act of murder or of punishment, depending on the circumstances.[114] Similarly, what would normally be an act of theft, such as picking up a piece of bread from the baker without paying, might cease to be theft when the agent needs the bread to support his own life or that of his family.[115] In such cases, the act is not "taking someone else's bread" but "taking bread" since according to Aquinas, under such circumstances all property is common. Theft is always wrong, but in some circumstances taking is not theft.

---

[111] Most of the material in this and the following comes from *In Sent*, lib. 2, d. 22, q. 2, art. 1, ad 4; d. 35, q. 1, art. 3 ad 3; *ST* I-II, q. 71, art. 5, ad 3; q. 88, art. 1, ad 2; II-II, q. 79, art. 3, ad 3; *DM* q. 2, art. 1, ad 11.

[112] *In Sent.*, lib. 3, d. 25, q. 2, art. 1, qc. 2 ad 3; *ST* II-II, q. 33, art. 2.

[113] *NE* 2.6.1107a10-12; *SLE*, lib. 2, lect. 7; *DM*, q. 2, art. 4c. For the wider context, see *ST* I-II, q. 18, art. 1–6; McInerny (1992), 75–86.

[114] *ST* II-II, q. 64, art. 2–3.   [115] *ST* II-II, q. 66, art. 7.

The negative precept against theft still holds, but it is not relevant to that time and the place.

Both affirmative and negative precepts are essential to moral reasoning and yet insufficient by themselves for determining a particular course of conduct. They regulate action insofar as they are or could be used in correct practical reasoning. They generally serve as major premises in a practical syllogism. For instance, someone might conclude that some bread should not be taken from the universal premise that "Theft should not be done" and the particular premise that "This taking of bread is theft." Or he might conclude that the bread should be taken from the universal premise that "Starving persons must be fed" and the particular premise that "Taking this bread is part of feeding starving persons." Negative precepts indicate what should always be avoided, but they do not indicate what should be done. Affirmative precepts indicate what ought to be done, but the agent needs to apply them in a particular situation.

Aquinas sheds light on practical reason by showing how its principles are in different ways similar to and different from those of speculative reason.[116] The primary principles of both practical and speculative reason are similar in that they are easily known and always yield true conclusions. In speculative reason, primary principles always hold and are known to everyone who grasps them by the habit of understanding. In practical reason, the primary principles are similarly known to everyone and always applicable. For instance, the first principle of speculative reason is that "One cannot affirm and deny at the same time."[117] This principle is presupposed in speculative reasoning even if it is not formulated or used in a speculative syllogism. Similarly, all practical reasoning presupposes that "Good should be done and pursued, and evil should be avoided."[118] However, agents typically do not formulate this principle or use it in a practical syllogism. Aquinas states that the first practical principles are known through "synderesis," which is the practical habit that corresponds to the habit of understanding by which first speculative principles are known.[119]

The secondary principles of practical reason are like those of speculative reason with respect to how they are known but unlike them in that they can lead to false conclusions. In speculative reason, secondary principles are deduced from primary principles, as can be seen clearly in geometry. They are known only to those who have learned the science. The secondary principles of practical reason, like those of speculative reason, are known to fewer people.

---

[116] *ST* I-II, q. 94, art. 2, 4, 6.   [117] "non est simul affirmare et negare." *ST* I-II, q. 94, art. 2c.

[118] "bonum est faciendum et prosequendum, et malum vitandum." *ST* I-II, q. 94, art. 2c.

[119] *ST* I, q. 79, art. 12.

Moreover, unlike the principles of speculative reason, they might yield incorrect conclusions when applied in some circumstances. A valid demonstrative speculative syllogism always has a true conclusion if its premises are true. A practical syllogism with a secondary precept as a premise does not always yield a true conclusion. For example, the secondary precept "Return borrowed items" indicates what should be done in most cases. Aquinas considers it to be a true premise. When combined with a premise such as "This axe is a borrowed item," it yields the conclusion that "This axe should be returned." But if a neighbor wants you to return her axe so that she can whack her parents with it, it would be wrong to return it at that time and place. The secondary precept about returning borrowed items in this case yields an incorrect conclusion. Since the conclusions of practical syllogisms involve particular actions, they are affected by an indeterminate number of circumstances. Moral principles that lead to conclusions whose truth can be changed by such circumstances are in this sense secondary principles.

There seems to be an order even among first practical principles. The very first practical principle, to do good and avoid evil, is known by everyone, but it is so general as to be unhelpful in most practical syllogisms. The basic precepts to love God and one's neighbor are the most easily known part of the natural law and in a sense contain or command the other precepts.[120] Even though our knowledge of them is weakened through sin, we can still know them without grace. However, the first – namely, the precept to love God – naturally, cannot be fulfilled without grace because of the effects of original sin.[121] Some readers today might think that since many people deny God's existence, such a moral principle cannot be universal. Aquinas is not suggesting that it is easy to grasp the Aristotelian *quia* demonstrations for God's existence or that everyone can do so. But he thinks that all morally healthy persons have some knowledge of God's existence.

The precept concerning love for one's neighbor includes the primary precept of the natural law that no harm should be done.[122] This principle is also universally known and without exception, even though there are many cases of virtuous acts that might be incorrectly described as harmful acts, such as fraternal correction, punishment, or even cases of performing acts that have unintended and harmful consequences. These basic precepts concerning God and one's neighbor are primary both in that they have no exceptions and in that they are easily known through their terms.

---

[120] *ST* I-II, q. 100, art. 5, ad 1; art. 6, ad 1.   [121] *ST* I-II, q. 109, art. 3.
[122] *ST* I-II, q. 100, art. 7c.

The precepts of the Decalogue, such as those against adultery, murder, and theft, are also primary precepts of the natural law in the sense that they are without exception and easily known.[123] But they are less easily known than the first practical principle and even posterior to the precepts concerning the love of God and neighbor. Aquinas should not be misunderstood as saying that there are two clearly distinct sets of natural law principles – namely, that of primary principles that are known to everyone and have no exceptions and that of secondary principles that are known to fewer people and have exceptions. Some principles are primary in that they have no exceptions and are easily known, and yet they might be unknown to many agents.[124] Aquinas states that all the precepts of the Decalogue, including that against theft, are primary precepts. The precept against theft is primary in that it has no exceptions and is presumably easily known. Nevertheless, according to Aquinas, it was in some way unknown to ancient Germans. Similarly, the prohibition of homosexual acts is also without exception and yet was unknown to those whom St. Paul described as idolaters. This prohibition of homosexual acts is not part of the Decalogue but is in some way derived from its prohibition of adultery. It is secondary because it is a derived principle, but it is not secondary in the sense that it has exceptions.

Aquinas's discussion of the Decalogue sheds much light not only on his understanding of the natural law's first principles but also on his account of the relationship between naturally known moral principles and supernatural revelation. Aquinas thinks that the whole Old or Mosaic law was revealed by God and can be divided into ceremonial, judicial, and moral precepts.[125] The ceremonial precepts were mainly for helping to prepare for Christ's coming and would now be sinful to follow.[126] The judicial precepts were for the public good of the Jewish community and need not be adopted by other groups, even though Aquinas thinks that they are eminently reasonable.[127] The moral precepts alone bind all humans both before and after Christ's coming.

Aquinas distinguishes between three kinds of revealed moral precepts.[128] First, some are common principles that are known to everyone without much consideration, such as the commandment to honor one's parents or the commandments against murder and theft. Others require judgment concerning circumstances and are known only to philosophers or to the wise, such as "Stand up in the presence of the hoary head, and honor the personage of old

---

[123] *ST* I-II, q. 100, art. 11.   [124] *ST* I-II, q. 94, art. 4c; art. 6c; *Sup. Rom.*, lib. 1, lect.7–8.
[125] *ST* I-II, q. 99, art. 2–4.   [126] *ST* I-II, q. 103, art. 3–4.   [127] *ST* I-II, q. 104, art. 3.
[128] *ST* I-II, q. 100, art. 1.

age."[129] They more determinately indicate what to do but are less easily and certainly known. Such precepts are derived from primary precepts, as this precept is derived from the commandment to honor one's parents. A third kind of precept requires revelation, such as the commandments against making an image of God or taking the Lord's name in vain. This third kind of precept seems to belong to the natural law as it pertains to good morals, even though it seems to presuppose revelation in some way. The precepts of the Decalogue for the most part, according to this threefold division, are primary precepts of the natural law.

Generally speaking, the moral precepts of the Old or Mosaic law belong to the natural law and either can be easily known to everyone or can be derived from such easily known principles by the wise. It is significant that such precepts are revealed, even though they can be known apart from revelation. For the most part, Aquinas states that God reveals moral principles in order for humans to have the knowledge they need to attain their end because this end exceeds human nature.[130] However, Aquinas also thinks that it can be difficult to know secondary natural-law precepts because of the influence of original and especially actual sin.[131] Original sin has an effect on knowledge, but it more seriously disorders the appetite than the intellect.[132] Perhaps more importantly, sinful habits affect the application of the commonly known moral precepts; more widely, human corruption leads to ignorance of many secondary precepts. Aquinas writes:

> Human reason concerning the moral precepts, with respect to those most common precepts of the natural law, cannot err in universal; however, because of the custom of sin, it is obscured in particular things that should be done. But concerning the other moral precepts, which are as it were conclusions deduced from the common principles of the natural law, the reason of many errs, such that certain things which are intrinsically evil, the reason of many judges to be licit.[133]

Although the precepts of the natural law can be known through reason, most humans without revelation will lack the knowledge that they need to live according to reason. The Germans who did not know the malice of theft and the idolaters who did not recognize that of homosexual acts seem to illustrate his

---

[129] "Coram cano capite consurge, et honora personam senis." Lev 19:32, quoted in *ST*, q. 100, art. 1c.
[130] *ST* I-II, q. 91, art. 4.   [131] *ST* II-II, q. 22, art. 1, ad 1; III, q. 60, art. 5, ad 3; q. 70, art. 2, ad 1.
[132] *ST* I-II, q. 109, art. 1–2.
[133] "Ratio autem hominis circa praecepta moralia, quantum ad ipsa communissima praecepta legis naturae, non poterat errare in universali, sed tamen, propter consuetudinem peccandi, obscurabatur in particularibus agendis. Circa alia vero praecepta moralia, quae sunt quasi conclusiones deductae ex communibus principiis legis naturae, multorum ratio oberrabat, ita ut quaedam quae secundum se sunt mala, ratio multorum licita iudicaret." *ST* I-II, q. 99, art. 2, ad 2.

statement that many will be unable to recognize the malice of intrinsically evil acts.

The Mosaic or Old law contains revealed moral principles that can be naturally known in much the same way that the Bible as a whole reveals not only truths that are inaccessible apart from revelation, such as the Trinity, but also truths that can be naturally known, such as God's existence. Without revelation such truths can be known but often they will not be. Although we can know some truths about God naturally, most people will not have the time or ability to know them without special help. Similarly, many truths about the natural law can be known by natural reason but are not so known.

Aquinas's view that there can be widespread moral ignorance raises a question concerning whether such moral ignorance is involuntary and consequently might excuse actions that are caused by it. The resulting false judgment about a particular act is the same as an erroneous conscience, since the conscience is the judgment about whether a particular act should or should not be done.[134] Aquinas's account of the erroneous conscience is influenced both by the tradition of civil and especially canon law and by Aristotle's account of agency, as mediated by Albert the Great (Lottin 1949, 55–92). Jurists had held that ignorance of the law under normal conditions does not excuse, but ignorance of particular facts does. According to Aristotle, ignorance of a particular circumstance can make an act involuntary, whereas ignorance of the universal does not.[135] For instance, a physician might give a patient poison that the physician erroneously mistakes for beneficial medicine. The ignorance concerning the poison can make the killing involuntary. But the physician might also be mistaken about the malice of murder. He might know that he is giving poison and murdering but think that murder is licit. Such ignorance about murder's malice does not excuse. Aquinas followed Albert the Great in identifying what Aristotle calls ignorance of the universal with what the jurists call ignorance of the law and what Aristotle names the ignorance of particular circumstances with what the jurists name ignorance concerning particular facts. According to Aquinas, ignorance concerning moral precepts is both an ignorance of the universal and an ignorance of the law and consequently does not excuse.[136]

Contemporary readers may find it confusing that Aquinas holds both that completely involuntary ignorance excuses and that ignorance of the natural law does not excuse. He consistently holds both because he thinks that ignorance

---

[134] *ST* I-II, q. 19, art. 5–6. See McInerny 1992, 90–98.

[135] *NE* 3.1.1110b27-1111a4; 3.5.1113b31-1114a2; *SLE*, lib. 3, lect. 3, 11.

[136] See especially *ST* II-II, q. 59, art. 4, ad 1.

of the natural law is at least in a broad way voluntary and therefore not involuntary in the complete way that would excuse the agent.[137] There can even be broadly voluntary ignorance about particulars that is not directly willed, as when someone might through negligence be ignorant of whether an item for sale is stolen. Such ignorance can be voluntary merely because of negligence. For Aquinas, ignorance of the basic moral rules is at the very least due to negligence. We all need to know the natural law to live well. Consequently, we are bound to know the basic principles of the natural law. Moreover, these basic principles are easily known. The ignorant have not taken sufficient effort to discover them or think about them.

The more widespread error involving the most common moral rules does not involve ignorance. It is that the correct rules are simply not used in moral reasoning. These rules are known but not applied. Passion can interfere with the use of principles. For instance, someone consumed by the desire for a tenth beer might drink too much while still knowing that drinking the tenth beer is drinking too much. She knows that it is bad but does not use the knowledge.

Like such easily known common precepts, derived precepts can be known and unused; but they can also be unknown. Aquinas indicates several reasons for such ignorance.[138] First, an agent might be deceived by defective arguments. Second, he might be ignorant due to "depraved custom and corrupt habits" (*propter pravas consuetudines et habitus corruptos*). The malice of theft and homosexual acts, according to Aquinas, would fall under this second category. His account of moral ignorance in this second context is not so much about moral philosophy but about ordinary nonphilosophical practical reasoning.

Aquinas tends not to mention philosophical error as a cause of culpable ignorance. Erroneous moral judgments typically result from other factors, such as passion, habits, and upbringing. These errors might be reflected in moral philosophy, but they do not seem to be caused by it. Unlike our own contemporaries, Aquinas rarely uses particular stories to illustrate examples of wider disagreements in moral philosophy. There are some areas of practical disagreement, such as over whether a judge can and should use privately obtained knowledge in deciding a case. But such disagreement is usually secondary. He and his interlocutors assume the malice of such acts as blasphemy, murder, theft, and adultery and that such malice has been recognized by many non-Christians, such as Aristotle and Cicero. Their disagreements are over how to explain and understand this malice.

---

[137] *ST* I-II, q. 6, art. 8c; q. 76, art. 2c; *DM*, q.3, art. 8c.   [138] *ST* I-II, q. 94, art. 6c.

On a more philosophical level, Aquinas did disagree with his contemporaries over such issues as whether ignorance of the moral law binds (Hoffmann 2012). For instance, if someone judges that a particular act of adultery is good, is she bound to commit this act in such a way that she sins if she refuses? Many of Aquinas's contemporaries thought that since the agent's reason was erroneous, the agent is not bound to perform the act. Aquinas replies that even if the act is bad, the agent's false judgment makes avoiding the act bad as well.[139] Consequently, the agent sins both by performing the act, since adultery is wrong, and by acting against it, since she judged that she should do it. The agent is in a dilemma according to which she sins either way. The original error concerning the moral precept is in some way voluntary and consequently so is the dilemma. The only way to escape this dilemma would be for her to correct her erroneous judgments. Aquinas assumes that such correction is possible and necessary for a virtuous life.

Aquinas develops his account of moral rules in the wider context of a moral theory that draws upon the Christian tradition, Aristotle, and other philosophers. Unlike some of our contemporaries, he sees no conflict between Aristotle's virtue ethics and a wider theory of moral reasoning that depends on moral rules. According to Aquinas, Aristotle mentions principles of practical reason that are the same as the natural law that is described by many non-Christians and Christians. The knowledge and use of the natural law originally comes from the natural habit of synderesis and is developed by prudence and the associated virtues.

Like Aristotle, Aquinas thinks moral reasoning depends on moral virtue in that prudence itself depends on the moral virtues and that these virtues themselves depend on prudence to produce their acts. Unruly passions prevent the application of the most basic moral principles. Vice and bad customs can corrupt the knowledge of derived moral principles. Prudence and the moral virtues are necessary for the consistent recognition and application of the relevant moral virtues. Consequently, an agent's errors in moral reasoning are not primarily errors in moral philosophy. On account of original sin and wide-spread vice, moral ignorance is widespread apart from revelation. Despite such ignorance, every rational agent has the ability to know basic moral principles. This knowledge is needed for morally virtuous action and consequently for the imperfect happiness of this life.

5 Conclusion

Aquinas's moral philosophy includes an account of the interdependence of happiness, the various moral virtues, and moral rules. Whereas some more

---

[139] *ST* I-II, q. 10, art. 6c and ad 3.

philosophers isolate and use only one or two of these elements, Aquinas thinks that they are interdependent. Ethics must be teleological insofar as happiness is the end of human action. It must include an account of the virtues since happiness is activity in accordance with virtue. In order to act virtuously, an agent must use and apply moral rules. Happiness can only be achieved through moral virtue, which can only be practiced by using moral rules.

Aquinas's basic approach is Aristotelian insofar as he thinks that most of Aristotle's writing on moral philosophy is true, both in its description of the moral life and in its wider methodology. But Aquinas's moral philosophy contains much more than what can be found in Aristotle. He takes material from other philosophical sources and Christian theology, and incorporates all of the material into his own moral philosophy. But Aquinas would not see this moral philosophy as peculiarly his or somehow belonging to him. He wishes to improve a science that he thinks was already developed by the previous philosophical and Christian tradition.

Aquinas's moral philosophy resists attempts to compartmentalize philosophy into one overarching theme or to isolate one philosophical tradition from another. For example, at first glance Aristotle's account of happiness as virtuous activity in this life seems incompatible with Augustine's Christian account of happiness as the beatific vision in the next life, as well as that of various pagan philosophers upon which Augustine himself drew. Aquinas plausibly holds that Aristotle and even other pagans were at least mostly correct in their description of moral activity and contemplation in this life but that this imperfect natural happiness is subordinate to the beatific vision. He thinks that previous thinkers all grasped at least some important truth about happiness and the ultimate end, even if they needed philosophical or theological supplementation and correction.

Moral philosophy should take into account a wide variety of moral and theoretical factors. Aquinas, like Aristotle, thinks that there are a variety of ways in which the natural happiness of this life can be achieved and that there are correspondingly many interconnected but specifically distinct moral virtues. Aquinas discusses far more virtues than Aristotle does, thanks to the way in which his thought is enriched by the writings of different Greek and Latin philosophers, as well as by the Christian tradition. Few if any writers have given a more complete account of the different moral virtues and their relations with each other than Aquinas does in the second part of the second part of the *Summa Theologiae*, in which he organizes all of morality around the theological virtues, the cardinal virtues, and the states of life.

As we have seen, the fact that Aquinas organizes his moral philosophy around the cardinal virtues rather than around commands or laws does not mean that he neglects moral rules. Virtuous action requires that the agent knows the universal propositions that direct action and consequently have the character of law. In some texts he describes the naturally known propositions as the "natural law." The virtuous agent needs to use such universal rules to arrive at the particular action-guiding knowledge upon which his virtue depends. These rules are necessary for him to achieve his ultimate end.

Later moral philosophers at times have separated one aspect of moral philosophy from another, such as ends, virtues, and rules. Moreover, some have advanced original theories that reject or are incompatible with those of previous philosophical traditions. Aquinas thinks that previous philosophers and theologians have all described at least some moral truths. He does not limit himself to any one author or tradition, but harmonizes much of what he finds in others. Aquinas's moral philosophy in this way is an instance of his wider intellectual approach, which is to incorporate whatever is valuable in previous and other traditions and to bring together aspects of the world and human behavior that others might separate.

Abbreviations

Works by Aquinas

DM	*Quaestiones disputatae De malo*
DV	*Quaestiones disputatae De veritate*
DVC	*Quaestio disputata De virtutibus in communi*
DVCard.	*Quaestio disputata De virtutibus cardinalibus*
DVCarit.	*Quaestio disputata De caritate*
In Sent.	*Scriptum super libros Sententiarum*
SLE	*Sententia libri Ethicorum*
In Met.	*Sententia super Metaphysicam*
SCG	*Summa contra Gentiles*
ST	*Summa theologiae*
I	First part of the *Summa theologiae*
I-II	First part of the first part of the *Summa theologiae*
II-II	Second part of the second part of the *Summa theologiae*
III	Third part of the *Summa theologiae*
Sup. Mat.	*Lectura super Matthaeum*
Sup. Rom.	*Lectura super Epistolam Pauli Apostoli ad Romanos*

In references to Aquinas's works that are written in the "disputed question" style, "c" refers to the body or main response of an article, "s.c." to the *sed contra* or considerations "on the other hand," while "ad" designates responses to initial objections. References to other texts can include "lib.," which indicates a book, "lect.," which signifies Aquinas's lecture on that book, and "dist.," which signifies a distinction number. Unless otherwise listed in the References, all citations from Aquinas's works are from the critical Leonine edition. A list of English translations can be found in Porro (2016): 412–417. Background on Aquinas's life and context can also be found in Porro's book, as well as in Torrell (2005).

On most of the cited texts from Aquinas, I have consulted over several years the relevant and often divergent commentaries by Thomas de Vio Cajetan, Francis Silvester de Ferrara, Bartholomew Medina, and John of St. Thomas, as well as Antoine Goudin's summary of Aquinas's philosophy. It is impossible for me to indicate precisely all of the ways in which I am indebted to them. Their work on Aquinas's ethics is unavailable in English. Special thanks to Steven Jensen for many helpful comments and to the two anonymous readers for Cambridge University Press.

Works by Aristotle

Met.	*Metaphysics*
NE	*Nicomachean Ethics*
Pol.	*Politics*

References

Aquinas Texts

Thomas Aquinas (1884–). *Opera omnia*. Rome: Commissio Leonina.

Thomas Aquinas (1927–1947). *Scriptum super libros Sententiarum*. 4 vols. Ed. Pierre Mandonnet and M. F. Moos. Paris: Lethielleux.

Thomas Aquinas (1951). *Super Evangelium S. Matthaei lectura* [Reportatio Petri de Andria]. 5th ed. Ed. R. Cai. Turin-Rome: Marietti.

Thomas Aquinas (1953). *Super epistolas S. Pauli lectura*. 2 vols. Ed. Raphael Cai. Turin: Marietti.

Thomas Aquinas (1953). *Quaestiones disputatae*. 2 vols. Ed. P. Bazzi, et al. Turin: Marietti. The *DVC, DVCard., DVCarit.* citations are all taken from vol. 2.

Thomas Aquinas (1964). *In duodecim libros Metaphysicorum Expositio*. Ed. M-R. Catala and R. Spiazzi. Turin: Marietti.

Other Sources

Bejcvy, Istvan (2005). "The Problem of Natural Virtue." In Istvan Bejcvy and Richard Newhauser, eds., *Virtue and Ethics in the Twelfth Century*, 133–154. Leiden: Brill.

Bejcvy, Istvan (2007). "The Cardinal Virtues in the Medieval Commentaries on the *Nicomachean Ethics*, 1250–1350." In Istvan Bejcvy, ed.,*Virtue Ethics in the Middle Ages: Commentaries on Aristotle's* Nicomachean Ethics, *1200–1500*, 199–221. Leiden: Brill.

Boyle, Leonard (2002). "The Setting of the *Summa Theologiae* of St. Thomas – Revisited." In Stephen J. Pope, ed., *The Ethics of Aquinas*, 1–16. Washington, D.C. : Georgetown University Press.

Cacouros, Michel (2003). "Le Traité pseudo-Aristotélicien *De virtutibus et vitiis*." In Richard Goulet, et al., eds., *Dictionnaire des philosophes antiques. Supplément*, 506–546. Paris: CNRS.

Feingold, Lawrence (2004). *The Natural Desire to See God according to St. Thomas and His Interpreters*. 2nd ed. Ave Maria, Fl.: Sapientia Press.

Finnis, John (2008). *Aquinas: Moral, Political, and Legal Theory*. Oxford: Oxford University Press.

Gallagher, David (1991). "Thomas Aquinas on the Will as Rational Appetite." *Journal of the History of Philosophy* 29, 559–584.

Goudin, Antoine (1680). *Philosophia Divi Thomae Dogmata*. Vol. 4: *Metaphysicam et Moralem Complectens*. Bologna.

Herdt, Jennifer A. (2013). "Aquinas's Aristotelian Defense of Martyr Courage." In Tobias Hoffmann, Jörn Müller, and Matthias Perkams, eds., *Aquinas and the* Nicomachean Ethics, 110–128. Cambridge: Cambridge University Press.

Hoffmann, Tobias (2008). "Albert the Great and Thomas Aquinas on Magnanimity." In Istvan Bejcvy, ed., *Virtue Ethics in the Middle Ages: Commentaries on Aristotle's* Nicomachean Ethics, *1200–1500*, 199–221. Leiden: Brill.

Hoffmann, Tobias (2012). "Conscience and Synderesis." In Brian Davies and Eleanore Stump, eds., *The Oxford Handbook of Aquinas*, 255–264. Oxford: Oxford University Press.

Hoffmann, Tobias (2013). "Prudence and Practical Principles." In Tobias Hoffmann, Jörn Müller, and Matthias Perkams, eds., *Aquinas and the* Nicomachean Ethics, 165–183. Cambridge: Cambridge University Press.

Houser, R.E. (2002). "The Virtue of Courage (IIaIIae, qq. 123–140)." In Stephen J. Pope, ed., *The Ethics of Aquinas*, 304–320. Washington, D.C.: Georgetown University Press.

Jensen, Steven (2010). *Good and Evil Actions: A Journey through Saint Thomas Aquinas*. Washington, D.C.: The Catholic University of America Press.

Jensen, Steven (2013). "Virtuous Deliberation and the Passions." *The Thomist* 77: 193–227.

Jensen, Steven (2015). *Knowing the Natural Law: From Precepts and Inclinations to Deriving Oughts*. Washington, D.C.: The Catholic University of America Press.

Lombardo, Nicholas E. (2018). "Emotion and Desire in the Summa Theologiae." In Jeffrey Hause, ed., *Aquinas's Summa Theologiae: A Critical Guide*, 111–130.

Lottin, Odon (1949). *Psychologie et morale aux xiie et xiiie siècles*. Vol. 3. Louvain and Gembloux : Mont-César and Ducolot.

MacIntyre, Alasdair (1992). "Plain Persons and Moral Philosophy: Rules, Virtues, and Goods." *American Catholic Philosophical Quarterly* 66 (1), 3–19.

MacIntyre, Alasdair (1999). *Dependent Rational Animals: Why Human Beings Need the Virtues*. Chicago, IL: Open Court.

McCluskey, Colleen (2000). "Happiness and Freedom in Aquinas's Theory of Action." *Medieval Philosophy and Theology* 9, 69–90.

McInerny, Ralph (1992). *Aquinas on Human Action: A Theory of Practice*. Washington, D.C.: The Catholic University of America Press.

McInerny, Ralph (1997). *Ethica Thomistica*. Rev. ed. Washington, D.C.: The Catholic University of America Press.

Müller, Jörn (2013). "Duplex Beatitudo: Aristotle's Legacy and Aquinas's Conception of Human Happiness." In Tobias Hoffmann, Jörn Müller, and

Matthias Perkams, eds., *Aquinas and the* Nicomachean Ethics, 52–71. Cambridge: Cambridge University Press.

Perkams, Matthias (2013). "Aquinas on Choice, Will, and Voluntary Action." In Tobias Hoffmann, Jörn Müller, and Matthias Perkams, eds., *Aquinas and the* Nicomachean Ethics, 72–90. Cambridge: Cambridge University Press.

Pieper, Josef (1966). *The Four Cardinal Virtues*. Trans. Richard and Clara Winston, Lawrence E. Lynch, and Daniel F. Coogan. Notre Dame, IN: University of Notre Dame Press.

Pinckaers, Servais (2005). *The Pinckaers Reader: Renewing Thomistic Moral Theology*. Ed. John Berkman and Craig Steve Titus. Trans. Mary Thomas Noble, et. al. Washington, D.C.: The Catholic University of America Press.

Pasquale, Porro (2016). *Thomas Aquinas: A Historical and Philosophical Profile*. Trans. Joseph G. Trabbic and Roger W. Nutt. Washington, D.C.: The Catholic University of America Press.

Torrell, Jean-Pierre (2005). *Aquinas's Summa: Background, Structure, and Reception*. Trans. Benedict M. Guevin. Washington, D.C.: The Catholic University of America Press.

Wallace, William A. (1996). *The Modeling of Nature: Philosophy of Science and Philosophy of Nature in Synthesis*. Washington, D.C.: The Catholic University of America Press.

White, Kevin (2013). "Pleasure: A Supervenient End." In Tobias Hoffmann, Jörn Müller, and Matthias Perkams, eds., *Aquinas and the* Nicomachean Ethics, 220–238. Cambridge: Cambridge University Press.

Elements in Ethics

Ben Eggleston
University of Kansas

Ben Eggleston is a professor of philosophy at the University of Kansas. He is the editor of John Stuart Mill, *Utilitarianism: With Related Remarks from Mill's Other Writings* (Hackett, 2017) and a co-editor of *Moral Theory and Climate Change: Ethical Perspectives on a Warming Planet* (Routledge, 2020), *The Cambridge Companion to Utilitarianism* (Cambridge, 2014), and *John Stuart Mill and the Art of Life* (Oxford, 2011). He is also the author of numerous articles and book chapters on various topics in ethics.

Dale E. Miller
Old Dominion University, Virginia

Dale E. Miller is a professor of philosophy at Old Dominion University. He is the author of *John Stuart Mill: Moral, Social and Political Thought* (Polity, 2010) and a co-editor of *Moral Theory and Climate Change: Ethical Perspectives on a Warming Planet* (Routledge, 2020), *A Companion to Mill* (Blackwell, 2017), *The Cambridge Companion to Utilitarianism* (Cambridge, 2014), *John Stuart Mill and the Art of Life* (Oxford, 2011), and *Morality, Rules, and Consequences: A Critical Reader* (Edinburgh, 2000). He is also the editor-in-chief of *Utilitas*, and the author of numerous articles and book chapters on various topics in ethics broadly construed.

About the Series

This Elements series provides an extensive overview of major figures, theories, and concepts in the field of ethics. Each entry in the series acquaints students with the main aspects of its topic while articulating the author's distinctive viewpoint in a manner that will interest researchers.

Cambridge Elements ≡

Elements in Ethics